D1258396

A SECOND YEAR'S
TALKS TO CHILDREN

Uniform with
ONE YEAR'S TALKS
TO CHILDREN
Fifty-two addresses
covering the whole
Christian Year

To
MAGDALENE ROSS JOHNSTON
Friend of Children

A SECOND YEAR'S
TALKS TO CHILDREN

By
EDGAR PRIMROSE DICKIE
Professor of Divinity, St. Mary's College
The University of St. Andrews

London : HODDER AND STOUGHTON, Limited

FIRST PRINTED . . . JANUARY 1943
REPRINTED . . . . MARCH 1943

Made and Printed in Great Britain for
Hodder and Stoughton Limited by
Hazell, Watson & Viney, Ltd., London and Aylesbury.

CONTENTS

CONTENTS

ACKNOWLEDGMENTS

THE author and publishers are grateful for permission to include the following copyright hymns : *Rise up, O men of God* (from *Enlarged Songs of Praise*), the Rev. Dr. W. P. Merrill and the Oxford University Press ; *Far round the world, Thy children sing their song* (from *Enlarged Songs of Praise*), Mr. Basil Mathews and the Oxford University Press ; *Dear Master, what can children do ?* and *Holy Spirit, hear us*, the National Sunday School Union ; *Be Thou my vision, O Lord of my heart*, Dr. Gilbert Hull and Messrs. Chatto & Windus ; *For the beauty of the earth* (from *Enlarged Songs of Praise*), the Estate of the late F. S. Pierpoint and the Oxford University Press ; *Father, whose will is life and good*, Mrs. E. F. Rawnsley ; *Just as I am, Thine own to be*, Messrs. James Clarke & Co., Ltd. ; *In the bleak Midwinter* (from the *Poetical Works of Christina Rossetti*), the author's representative and Messrs. Macmillan & Co., Ltd.

In any case where we have failed to reach the owner of the copyright, or the necessary permission has been overlooked, we offer our apologies.

The play on page 144 has already been successfully performed by quite young children. Church societies and youth organisations wishing to produce it may obtain permission, without fee, by writing to the publishers, Messrs. Hodder and Stoughton, Ltd., St. Hugh's School, Bickley, Kent.

I

ARITHMETIC LESSON

(NEW YEAR)

" Teach us to number our days."—PSALM XC. 12.

HERE we have two sums. One is to count the number of days you have lived already : you can easily find the answer to that one. Be sure to count an extra day for Leap Year ; and, if you like, we shan't count that dreadful day when everything seemed to go wrong : you fell asleep again after you were wakened, you spilled the milk at breakfast and in your haste broke your shoe-lace and mended it with a granny-knot ; you were nearly late for school, and then were so hot and bothered in the history-class that you mixed up Queen Elizabeth and Queen Victoria, and almost had Shakespeare writing about the Indian Mutiny. Perhaps we should forget that day. The other sum is to find the number of days you have still to live, but no one knows the answer to that, except God.

This is a time for counting. God gives a lesson in arithmetic. At the beginning of a New Year He teaches us to number our days.

You know that we usually count them by means of a calendar. Sometimes it is a ' tear-off.' When the day is finished you tear off the slip of paper and put it in the salvage-bag. It passes beyond your control. Your day will go on acting for you. Just as the slip of paper may go on to make wads for cartridges or do some other useful work of which you may know nothing at all, so your day will go on and on, helping people or hindering people, long after you have forgotten all about it. But the 'tear-off' calendar also reminds you that the day can't be called back again. When it's gone, it's gone. Time doesn't stand still. It is true there was once a poet who wanted Time to stop a little. He thought it was like a gipsy on the roads. Would it not be splendid if you could get him to stay with you for a night or two and to put up his tent in your garden?

> Time, you old gipsy man,
> Will you not stay,
> Put up your caravan
> Just for one day?

But not even a poet can make him halt.

Some of these calendars have jokes on them, a joke for each day. Even when you put the slip away, you remember the joke and share it with others. And God likes every day to bring you some happy memory.

Others have texts on them. When the slip is gone, you remember the text. God likes you every day to learn something new about Him. Even though you go on learning about Him to the end of the sum, something new every morning, you will not come to the end.

A friend has sent me a new kind of calendar. When the first day of the month is finished you turn a small screw and a red line creeps out and strokes off the day. Each day it creeps a little bit farther and strokes out another day. It makes you think how swiftly the days run past. You seem to hear Time galloping up behind you in a chariot; and you try hard to get something useful done before he catches up on you.

> At my back I always hear
> Time's wingéd chariot hurrying near.

But what I like best of all about this calendar is that, if you go on winding after the month is done, suddenly all the red lines disappear out of sight, and there are the days standing all ready to begin again!

Is that not a fine thing? We waste so many of our days. We do nothing with them. We make nobody happier in them. And they are all stroked out and finished. And then—then Jesus can brush His hand over them and there is a new, fresh set of days in which we can do better.

HYMN

> March on, my soul, with strength,
>   March forward, void of fear;
> He who hath led will lead,
>   While year succeedeth year;
> And as thou goest on thy way,
> His hand shall hold thee day by day.

"NO COMPLIMENTS"

" Salute no man by the way."—LUKE x. 4.

IT seems a strange piece of advice for Jesus to give to the disciples, and I am sure He did not mean them to forget about being polite and courteous. Greetings by the way are a sign of friendliness and good manners. Some of them are very beautiful. In parts of Switzerland you will hear the peasants salute one another when they meet with the words, " *Grüss Gott!* "—" May God greet you ! " In Uganda, the African who sees a friend busy at his morning's work greets him with the fine words, " Many thanks ! Well done ! " In the East the familiar greeting was, " Peace be upon you ! " and it was answered by the words, " And upon you be peace ! "

Nevertheless, there are times when we have to think of something far more important than courtesy. In the summer of 1940, when it was thought quite likely that Germans might attempt to land in lonely parts of Britain, we were warned against giving polite information to strangers. It was suggested that, if you were asked by some unknown person to direct him on his way, the best reply was to say, " I'm sorry, I can't tell you ; I'm a parachutist myself." Even the polite people of the East recognise that there are times when politeness must go by the board. The Jews were told not to turn aside to greet people if, for example, they were mourning for some lost friend. And two things were specially mentioned which, though important in themselves, were not to be allowed to interrupt those who were at prayer : the first to salute a king, the second to uncoil a serpent from the foot !

First of all, Jesus meant to say to His disciples, "Do not try to please everyone—or you will end by pleasing no one, and getting nothing done." If you have to choose between politeness and duty, choose duty.

There was once a man who had two friends whom he liked to please. The man's hair was beginning to turn white, and one of the friends didn't like this. So, every time they met, he pulled out a dozen or two of the white hairs. But the other friend had hair that was altogether white, and every time *he* met him he would pull out a handful of *black* hairs to make his friend's head more like his own. In the end the poor man had neither black nor white hair left. He tried to please both, and he ended by pleasing no one.

Do not think only of pleasing people, Jesus said ; do what is right.

In the second place, He meant the disciples to remember that the time is short : it must not be wasted. It may take only a moment to say, "Good morning," but in the East it may take a much longer time to be polite. If once you stop, you have to ask for everyone in the family, and all their friends and their friends' families, and their friends' families' friends. A whole morning might be spent courteously and bashfully marking time. The same is true of many parts of Africa. When Miss Mary Slessor went to a meeting of the chiefs, she knew that they would talk for several hours before they came to the real business, and she used therefore to take her knitting with her and work away till they had finished their greetings and were ready for the real work. In that way, she knitted hundreds of pairs of stockings during palavers.

Be careful of your time, Jesus was saying : there is much work to be done.

The third consideration is the most important. You know the custom of the Army to pay compliments on the march. When a battalion meets, let us say, a very senior officer, the men " march to attention." They carry their rifles at the slope and the band plays ; they stop all talking and singing and whistling. And, when they are passing the great man, they all turn their heads and eyes towards him as a mark of respect. And that is fine, polite, and wholesome. But there are times when this does not happen. When the men are doing a long march in order to go straight into battle, the order is sent out, by the senior officer himself, " No compliments on the march." That is just the same as the words, " Salute no man by the way." Why not ? Because the business on which they are going is far more important than compliments. The men are not to be tired nor hindered nor delayed even by the usual graces and courtesies. They are too busy and too earnest.

" The King's business requires haste."

Hymn

Rise up, O men of God !
  Have done with lesser things ;
Give heart and soul and mind and strength
  To serve the King of kings.

IN THE BUCKLE

" He was a mighty hunter before the Lord."—GENESIS x. 9.

PERHAPS you know the splendid stories about hunting in Mr. Kipling's *Jungle Book*. There is one about a boy and a black panther who went tracking together. They followed the trail for a long distance in the moonlight and then they lost it under the trees. It was the panther who found it again. He knew the trick. When the trail disappeared, the panther flung himself forward with one superb bound as far as ever he could. That is the most important thing for a panther to remember in tracking—to go forward without leaving your own footmarks to confuse the trail. You must read these stories about hunting in the hottest parts of the world.

There is another story in the same book about hunting in the coldest part of the world, among the Eskimos in Baffin Land. These people live next door, as it were, to the North Pole. For nine months of the year there is nothing but ice and snow. And —what is much worse—for six of these months the sun does not shine. Here there lived a boy, fourteen years old, who wanted to be a great hunter like his father. But the grown men laughed at him and said, " Wait till you have been in the buckle." You wonder what that means ?

This is what happened. When the boy was old enough to go out hunting for seals in the darkness of the long winter, he sent his own special dog looking far and wide for the hole in the ice where a seal would come up to breathe. Then he built a wall of snow to keep off the bitter wind, and sat down to wait till the seal should come. Ten, twelve, even twenty hours he had to wait, and all the time his eyes had to be fixed on a little mark he had made just beside the hole, so that, as soon as the seal showed its nose, he could strike downwards with his harpoon. And now he knew what the buckle meant. In the long wait, he wanted desperately to move his legs about. (You know how they get cramped, sitting even for a minute or two in one position; how hard it is to sit still even for a little. But he had to sit perhaps the best part of a whole day.) Even a twitch of his foot would make a noise on the ice, and the seal, with his quick ears, would know that someone was waiting there for him. And so the boy had tied his feet together with a buckle. That is the hardest part of an Eskimo's life, to sit still, hour after hour, with nothing to do but just sit still and watch, with no excitement at all. He could never do it without the buckle.

But the Eskimos have learned to do this. They know how to keep themselves in check. And people say that they are the gentlest race in all the world. An Eskimo is hardly ever known to lose his temper.

That is what we call self-control. You know what getting out of control means. If you see a horse galloping along the road with a lorry bumping and swaying behind it, perhaps crashing at last into a wall, you know that horse has got out of control. If a motor-car is going downhill and the brakes refuse to act, it is out of control. They are dangerous to themselves and to everyone else.

And so are we if we cannot control ourselves; if we want our own way and will allow nothing else; if we lose our tempers and begin using angry words to everybody. We are out of control. What we need is a buckle—to tie up our tongues and to tie up our tempers till the danger is past.

Our buckle is within. Whenever we feel that we are going to be angry, to lose our tempers, to get out of hand and be a danger and a nuisance to all around, we need to say quietly, " Let me remember that I am a child of Jesus. I must learn His gentleness."

HYMN

We are but little children weak,
    Nor born in any high estate ;
What can we do for Jesus' sake,
    Who is so high and good and great ?

When deep within our swelling hearts
    The thoughts of pride and anger rise,
When bitter words are on our tongues,
    And tears of passion in our eyes;

Then we may stay the angry blow,
    Then we may check the hasty word,
Give gentle answers back again,
    And fight a battle for our Lord.

POCKETS

" Earneth wages to put it into a bag with holes."—HAGGAI i. 6.

ONCE upon a time I was mistaken for a smuggler. I was landing at a port in the English Channel and had passed all my baggage through the customs ; but, at the barrier, where they look to see that all your things are properly marked, an official startled me by asking suddenly, " What have you got in your pocket, sir ? " In my overcoat pocket there was a big, untidy bulge. It was really a bunch of news-papers for reading in the train, but he thought it might be something I shouldn't have. You mustn't, for instance, bring dogs into the country without special precautions. And perhaps he thought that this was a puppy that I was trying to smuggle through.

" What have you got in your pocket, sir ? " The question made me think, and, whenever I was alone, I turned out my pockets to see all that was in them. And I was surprised to see the curious collection of stuff. You should try this experiment.

What have *you* in your pocket ? This is perhaps a question specially for boys. (Where *do* girls carry things ? Perhaps, like the sailors, they carry them in their hats.) And I don't mean your Sunday pockets —they are specially cleared. Probably you have only your collection and perhaps a peppermint for the sermon. But in your weekday pockets ? Very likely a queer mixture ; and the strange thing is that you can tell what kind of person you are by your pocket.

1. Perhaps you have some packets of foreign stamps; and it is good to gather interesting, handsome things, and to learn through them some history and geography. But these are mostly for your own amusement.

2. Perhaps string and a knife and some safety-pins. That is better; for you can often use these for helping others.

Remember that your *mind* is a wonderful pocket. Be careful what you put in it. We can tell what you are, not by your Sunday mind, perhaps, but by your weekday mind.

3. There are things that shouldn't be there. Toffee, perhaps, if you are lucky? That is precious these days, but it shouldn't be loose in your pocket. It makes everything else sticky, and it's not too good for the toffee. In your mind you may have nasty thoughts about other people. If you have, you can't put anything good and fine in beside them.

4. Another thing you shouldn't have—a hole! It may be small, but it can make all the rest useless. The text says that some men earn wages to put into a bag with holes. They draw their pay on Saturday and drop it into their pocket and on the way home it falls out through a hole. And they feel very foolish when twenty or thirty honest little boys come running after them, saying, "Did you drop this, sir?" "And this, sir?" "And this, sir?" . . .

You can have holes in your mind too. Then all the good things that God says to you go in at one ear and out at the other.

And the hole goes on getting bigger. First a three-penny-bit drops through, then a sixpence, then a shilling. . . . If it went on mounting like that I believe the mathematics books would tell you that in a year you would have lost enough money to pay for the whole war for a day.

So it is too in your mind. There is a little hole called LAZINESS ; a little hole called ENJOYING MYSELF ; and a little hole called TEMPER. Out go all the fine things that God has said.

But the hole can be mended. You can't mend it yourself. You try to mend your pocket and you know what happens. You just draw it together, and, the first time you put in your hand, your finger goes right through again. You have to run to your mother or your big sister.

When we find holes in our mind—Laziness, Enjoying Myself, Temper—there is only One who can mend them, and that is Jesus. Take them straight to Him.

HYMN

Tell me the story slowly,
　　That I may take it in,—
That wonderful redemption,
　　God's remedy for sin.

Tell me the story often,
　　For I forget so soon ;
The early dew of morning
　　Has passed away at noon.

Yes, and, when that world's glory
　　Shall dawn upon my soul,
Tell me the old, old story—
　　' Christ Jesus makes thee whole.'

19

LAND AHEAD!

" At midnight the shipmen deemed that they drew near to some country."
—ACTS xxvii. 27.

WHAT made the sailors think that they were coming near some land?

You have heard people speak of the *Five Senses*—seeing and hearing and smelling and tasting and touching. It must have been by one of these. The usual way is by seeing. A ship has been on a long voyage, with never a sight of land for days and weeks. Then, perhaps, someone catches sight of a branch with berries on it floating past. Or suddenly, from the look-out man there is a shout of " Land! " Through his telescope he has seen a thin line on the horizon, and he knows that they are drawing near to some country. But in this case it wasn't through the eyes. It was midnight; and it was cloudy: there were no stars nor light of any kind to be seen. I think it was probably by the ears. The storm was raging all around, but in the midst of it a trained sailor heard something different. He shouted, " Listen! " And, above the roaring of the storm, those who were old sailors heard another sound far away but quite distinct, the noise of breakers, the sea beating on some line of coast.

Sometimes, I believe, you can tell by your nose that you are approaching land. If you are going in a ship away out to the East of the world, you may find, when you are still a long way from any land, a beautiful scent in the air. It is the fragrance of flowers and spices growing on the shore.

After eyes, ears, nose, there is the mouth. Sometimes you can tell by taste that you are coming near land. Perhaps there is a great river running into the sea. For many miles out the water of the river will freshen the salt of the sea. Dip your hand overboard and you can tell by tasting that you are coming near to some country.

Lastly, there is the sense of touch. The sailors in the story tried this. They let down a sounding-line to see if they could touch the bottom. Perhaps you are all very good swimmers, but, if some of you are only fairly good, I expect you have tried this way. I know, when I am swimming, I always find it a very comfortable thing every now and then to let down my toe just to feel that the land is still there ; to make sure that I haven't gone too far out.

It is possible, too, to tell that you are approaching land—not by the eyes, nor the ears, nor the nose, nor by taste, nor by touch, but—by something away inside us : by the mind. A man can sit in the chart-room and calculate, by map and compass, where the ship is now and how near it is to land.

There is another way. Did you notice, in verse twenty-six, that *Paul* was the first to be certain that they were coming safe to land. All the rest were hungry and hopeless and terrified. Paul alone was calm and confident. And yet he was not an expert sailor like some of the others. How then did he know ? Not by the five senses. Not by his mind.

But by something farther in still, by his soul. He had been praying; asking God about it all; and he knew now that it was all right: not by any of the senses, but by this deeper and truer thing, his soul, where God had spoken to him. This sense of the soul is called *Faith*. The name doesn't matter, but I want you to think of this sixth sense. It can tell you many things of which the others know nothing. It is this sense that tells you about Heaven. No one has ever seen Heaven; no one has touched it. But we know about that country by our souls. Men have asked God about it in the prayers of their souls, and He has said, Yes; you are drawing near to this country.

HYMN

Jesu, Lover of my soul,
  Let me to Thy bosom fly,
While the nearer waters roll,
  While the tempest still is high:
Hide me, O my Saviour, hide,
  Till the storm of life is past;
Safe into the haven guide;
  O receive my soul at last.

6

WRITING TO LAST

" Graven with an iron pen and lead on the rock for ever."—JOB xix. 24.

Do you ever look at the newspapers? If you do, you will notice that the headings—the bits at the top —are sometimes written in small letters and sometimes in big letters. If there is something very important it is printed in huge letters. During the last war there was so much that was important to tell about that the letters kept on getting bigger and bigger until, in some countries, a law had to be passed saying that they were not to be more than three inches long. Wise men felt that people might become frightened if they saw these huge letters: they might imagine that the end of the world had come.

Job had something very important to write: he wanted the writing to last for ever, and he thought the only way was to carve it out of the rock and then to pour in lead. (You know how we write unimportant things in pencil; more important ones in ink. Very important ones we type; and, if we think they are of the utmost importance, we print them.) Job did not know how to print, so he wanted to write what he had discovered on the rock.

Once, during the war between the Greeks and the Persians, Themistocles was in command of the Greek fleet. With the enemy were serving some sailors who were really Greek, Ionians; and, just as to-day we send messages to our friends in countries occupied by the enemy by radio and by leaflets dropped from the air, Themistocles decided to make contact with these people in the enemy's navy. He chose the fastest ships and sent them to all the harbours in the district to cut huge inscriptions in the rock, which would be read next day by the Ionians. In gigantic letters they saw, carved deep in the rock-face :

YE DO WRONG TO FIGHT AGAINST YOUR OWN FATHERS.
COME OVER TO OUR SIDE.
IF STOPPED, THEN FIGHT BACKWARDLY.
DELAY ! SABOTAGE !

Job had found such an important thing to say that he felt he must write it where the whole world could read. His message was that, in spite of his terrible illness, he had discovered that God was always looking after him.

Sometimes we write to-day with an iron pen on the rock and pour lead into the letters, as, for example, in putting the names on our war-memorials : we want these names to be remembered for ever.

Jesus once wanted to write a great piece of news so that it would be read for ever. It was the same great tidings that Job spoke about. It can be written in three words : *God is Love*. Jesus did not write it on a rock (He wrote only once that we know of ; and that was in the sand) ; He wrote it by dying on the Cross for us. We look upwards now and see the message standing out clear against the sky. Nineteen hundred years it has been there, but the writing has never faded. People are reading it all the world over.

Hymn

(We sing the praise of Him who died)

Inscribed upon the Cross we see,
  In shining letters, ' God is love ' ;
He bears our sins upon the Tree ;
  He brings us mercy from above.

7

LOST PROPERTY

" He was lost and is found."—LUKE xv. 32.

IT would be interesting to make a list of all the things
we have ever lost and then to have them all gathered
together in one big field. There would be pencils
and pens and books and bats and balls; and over
there in the corner, perhaps, there would be a railway-
engine and some coaches, because we once lost a train.
Often we have lost games : they would go down on
the list. Sometimes we have lost our way. Then
think how often we lose time. And, when it comes
to examinations at school, we lose our memories ; we
get excited and lose our heads (perhaps, then, our
heads would have to go into another corner of the
field) ; we lose marks and we lose prizes. Think too
of all the lost opportunities. And sometimes, I'm
afraid, we even lose our tempers.

In every big city there is an interesting place where
lost things are found again. It is called the ' Lost
Property Office.' (If you lose your temper you
won't find *it* there. You must find *that* for yourself.
And lost opportunities are almost never found again.)
In this office there is money which has been lost.
Even in Edinburgh, the capital of a country where
people are supposed to look well after money, £100
is lost every month and taken to this office. There
you will see spades and buckets that have been used
on the sands not long ago. There are toys, tricycles,

and fairy cycles. (Fancy losing a fairy cycle! But there it is!) And children are not the only ones who lose things. You will see gas-masks and prams and false teeth, and a special book for lost dogs, and for lost parrots, and for lost cats. The other day there was handed in a lost box of kippers. And there are whole forests of walking-sticks and umbrellas. One day a lady called to ask about her umbrella. It was there, and she was going off with it when the official in charge called her back. "You have to sign this," he said, "before you go." She signed a receipt for her umbrella and was at the door when he called her back again. "What is it this time?" she asked. "This time," the official said, "it is your umbrella. You have forgotten it again." So soon!

Perhaps the most interesting point to notice is the things that are *not* there. Big drums, of course, and elephants, and road-rollers and church-organs are hardly ever found in the office. And you will probably find that there are no children there. They may come sometimes to the Lost Property Office, but they go away again at once. Why is that? It is because they are precious to someone. They are claimed immediately. People may forget all about their umbrellas or their prams or even their teeth, but they can't forget about the baby.

Jesus tells us three stories about Lost Property. The first tells about a sixpence which fell on the floor and couldn't be found: the woman who had lost it took a candle and swept the whole house until she found it. The second is about a sheep that wandered away and got lost. And the shepherd went after it, over hill and over dale, searching everywhere till he heard it bleating, made his way to it, and brought it home on his shoulder. The third is the most beautiful story—how a boy was lost. It was his own fault. He wanted to have a good time. His father warned him and tried to keep him at home, but no! off he went. It was only when he was starving and terribly home-sick that he went back. His father said nothing about the past, but just took him in again and made him very welcome and very happy. Jesus would have us understand that God does not forget us, however far away we have wandered. We may be lost, but we are never lost to Him.

Very often, in the early days of long-distance flying, we used to hear of airmen being lost, setting off perhaps to fly the Atlantic and never being heard of again. But it happened sometimes that we *did* hear of them. We couldn't find them at once, and they couldn't get back of themselves, but they could speak to us. They had a wireless-set, and they could tell where they were and what they were most in need of. That is perhaps the most useful thing you can have when you are lost.

When you have wandered away, like that boy who went off to enjoy himself, this ' wireless-set ' is the only thing that will get you back. We call it Prayer—sending a message to God, telling Him what you need; and telling Him that you want to come back. Jesus is waiting for that message, to come for you.

" I came into the world," He said, " to seek and to save that which was lost."

HYMN

Come, let us to the Lord our God
    With contrite hearts return ;
Our God is gracious, nor will leave
    The desolate to mourn.

Our hearts, if God we seek to know,
    Shall know Him and rejoice ;
His coming like the morn shall be,
    Like morning songs His voice.

8

TRUMPET-BLOWING

" The sound of the trumpet."—THE BIBLE, frequently.

LET us look at some uses of the trumpet. A friend once told me a good railway-compartment story. A small boy was proud of a new trumpet he had for a birthday-present and was blaring away with all the might of his lungs. The father was afraid that he was disturbing the rest of the passengers, so he took the trumpet and hid it. Then there was a dreadful noise of crying and temper. At last the mother said, " Give him it back : it'll keep him quiet." Quiet ! Perhaps, though, she was quite right. He couldn't be much noisier one way than the other, and it is better to listen to a happy noise than to a cross one.

Jesus has a delightful story about a trumpet. Here is a man, He says, who wants to give something to a beggar. But he can't do it quietly. He must send his servant to buy a trumpet. Then he makes him walk in front, blowing as loudly as he can. Soon the whole town is roused. The rumour goes round that a very rich man is going to make presents. " A hundred pounds at least," says one. And another, " I think it must be a thousand. All that blowing means a lot of money." And one shouts to another, " Come on ! There's ten pounds for every one." Then, when they are all gathered, the rich man calls out the beggar, gives him a penny, and goes off with his servant and his trumpet. And the people say,

" All that commotion about a penny ! " That's not the way, Jesus says. If you want to be kind, do it quietly ; and He tells another story, a story about Heaven. The kindest people there get a reward because they were once good to a poor man. God says to them, Do you not remember ? And they say, I had forgotten all about it. But God had remembered, though it was done without any noise, and without anyone else knowing.

When you wish to do a good action, don't blow a trumpet to call attention. Just do it. We have a proverb which says, " Blowing your own trumpet." It just means making a great fuss to tell the world how clever or how kind or how wonderful you are.

That great man, Marshal Foch, who was Commander-in-Chief of the Allied Forces during the last war, tells how his brother came dancing home from school one day, with a prize, crying out, " See how clever I am ! " " My child," said his mother, " cleverness that must be mentioned does not exist." Neither of them ever forgot that lesson.

To-day we have very few trumpets in the streets, but we have something like them. We have motor-horns. And a little book has been written for the guidance of motorists, telling them how to use their horns. It is called " The Highway Code," and is just a book of good manners. Remember, it says, that your horn is a request, not a threat. " Blow it gently, to say, ' Excuse me : may I come past ? ' " Don't blow it with a roar and a scream, saying, " Get out of my way ! " These are manners for motorists. But they are also manners for all of us.

To be gentle—that is more than good manners : it is the law of Jesus. " Learn of Me, for I am meek and lowly in heart."

HYMN

What grace, O Lord, and beauty shone
    Around Thy steps below ;
What patient love was seen in all
    Thy life and death of woe !

One with Thyself, may every eye
    In us, Thy brethren, see
The gentleness and grace that spring
    From union, Lord, with Thee.

9

ON KEEPING QUIET

" Be still and know that I am God."—PSALM xlvi. 10.

IT's very difficult to be still. In drill, one of the hardest lessons to learn is to stand at attention perfectly still on parade, while you are being inspected. A specially hard part for girls and boys in being still is to keep from talking. It is just when you are told to be quiet that you remember a hundred and one important things that you must say.

And I suppose it must be very seldom indeed that we have complete and absolute silence. Even on the quietest night you have only to listen attentively for a little while and you will hear all kinds of faint noises like the rustle of the wind in the trees, the chirp of birds, the movement of small animals in the grass, the sound of running water far off in a hidden stream. Once, I believe, I came as near as possible to complete silence. It was in a hospital in London where they test people's hearing. They must have absolute stillness for their examinations, so the room is lined with cork on walls and floor, and there is a strong double door which shuts out all noise from outside. The quietness is uncanny : I had never known anything quite like it before ; you felt that you were hearing your own heart beating and your blood running along your veins.

There are times when we *must* be quiet, if we want to hear God speaking to us. There are times when

He speaks only in a whisper. I remember standing once in a trench during a war, when it was impossible to hear anything but the terrific roar of the guns. There was a sudden silence, while the artillery " lifted the barrage " forward, and in that silent moment you could hear, far away up in the blue sky, a skylark singing. Then you knew that God was there in spite of all the foolishness and hatred of men.

Once upon a time an old prophet thought that he had lost God, and he set out to try to find Him again in a holy mountain far off from home. Like Elijah he expected to find God in a peal of thunder or an earthquake. Nothing happened. There was not even a breath of wind. But suddenly at his feet a little tuft of moss quietly opened, and a violet sprang up. He knew that God was there. Then he recalled that just as he left home his daughter had run up to him with a handful of violets. They grew at his own door : he saw them every day ; he had no need to come all this way to see them. But he needed to be still.

Some people imagine that they are not getting on at all unless they are making a noise. A king once wrote to the Spartans (who were famous for their quietness—they never used two words where one would do), " If I enter Sparta I shall put everything to the fire and sword." He hoped to frighten them by the noise he made. " If I enter Sparta I shall put everything to the fire and sword." The Spartans wrote back : " IF."

It isn't the noisy ones who are the strong ones. You always know there is something wrong in a machine if it makes a noise. (You know that well from your bicycle.) When an engine is running powerfully and well it is silent. The stars make no noise as they spin round. But their very silence is a great song of praise to God who made them.

> What though in solemn silence all
> Move round this dark terrestrial ball;
> What though no real voice nor sound
> Amidst their radiant orbs be found:
> In reason's ear they all rejoice,
> And utter forth a glorious voice,
> For ever singing as they shine:
> The hand that made us is divine!

If you want to be strong like the stars, you must be quiet and think about God.

You must do that too if you want to be pure. In Switzerland there is a lake where you may see a curious thing. Into it there flows a river, all muddy from the rocks and earth from the mountains. But it flows out again pure and lovely. The mud has had time to sink down, while the lake was still. So, if you are quiet, and think about God, all your unlovely thoughts sink away down, and you come out like the stream, pure and beautiful.

There are some good people who make this silence the chief part of their Church service—to be still and wait for God. And, as we might expect, they are strong and they are pure; strong like the silent stars, and pure as the water that has lost all its sand. They are so strong that, even when men persecuted them, they were not hurt. They are so pure that, when they come into a great smoky city for a conference—

the Quakeress girls in their clean, sweet dresses—they are like beautiful lilies in the dark streets.

You do not need to go to Church to be still. Jesus loved to go for quiet and peace into some desert place beside the sea, or into the lonely hills of Galilee, to be still and to know that God was very near. We can do that too. In our prayers every morning and night—and in the middle of the day too—that is the time when we can be still and know that God is there. But perhaps it is on Sunday that we can do it most easily. That is why we have one day in the week without work and without noisy games, when we want everything to be as quiet as possible. Then we can be still and know that God is there.

HYMN

(Dear Lord and Father of mankind)

O Sabbath rest by Galilee !
　　O calm of hills above,
Where Jesus knelt to share with Thee
The silence of eternity,
　　Interpreted by love !

With that deep hush subduing all
　　Our words and works that drown
The tender whisper of Thy call,
As noiseless let Thy blessing fall
　　As fell Thy manna down.

Drop Thy still dews of quietness,
　　Till all our strivings cease ;
Take from our souls the strain and stress,
And let our ordered lives confess
　　The beauty of Thy peace.

ROOM TO PLAY

" And the Lord God planted a garden."—GENESIS ii. 8.

Two men were standing in a deep, narrow ditch, up to their knees in mud. They didn't dare to raise their heads above the top of it, because they were in the middle of a war. There was not a flower or a tree anywhere near them. Every green and growing thing had been blown to bits by shell-fire. One of the men asked his friend, " What will be the first thing you do when you get home after the war is finished?" He thought that the answer might be, " Have a good breakfast," for they had had nothing that morning but hard biscuits. Or, he thought, the answer might be, " I'll have a good game of football," or " I'll just sit by the fire and get properly warm for once." But it wasn't. The answer was, " I'll go and dig in the garden."

That man was right. I'm not quite sure about the digging ; but, among all the jolly things in this world, a garden is hard to beat.

Who, do you think, first thought of making a garden? Some say that the first garden was made by a boy and a girl. They weren't allowed to play in the house, because of the noise. Whenever they began to play a specially noisy game, the baby seemed to choose that moment to go to sleep ; and he had a pleasant habit, even when he wasn't sleeping, of putting one finger on his lips and murmuring, " Hush ;

baby's as'eep ! " Besides, there wasn't nearly enough room in the house for all the best games ; so they set to, and made a garden outside. They put in apple-trees and gooseberry-bushes and black-currants. (That was the boy's idea !) The girl wanted some roses ; so they put them in too.

Others say, No ; that wasn't the beginning of gardens. But this was the way of it : Once upon a time there were no houses, and families moved about with tents—a kind of camping-holiday all their lives ! Then they settled down, tired of camp-life. The father built a house. The mother made a garden. The boy planted apple-trees, and gooseberry-bushes, and black-currants. And the girl planted roses. So they never again wanted to move about and live in tents.

Now, you and I know, because we read it in the Bible, that the first person to think about a garden was God. We find, in the second chapter of the Bible, that " The Lord God planted a garden," and we find also that He loved to walk in it in the cool of the evening. Not only that, but He looks after *all* the gardens. We can put in seeds and flowers, but nothing will happen if God doesn't send His rain and His sunshine.

Have *you* a garden ? Remember that God walks in it. When you see a new flower in the morning, say to yourself, " God has been here during the night."

Have you *not* a garden ? Yes, you have. There it is, outside. All the world is God's garden. He planted it, and put in the flowers and the trees,

Wherever you go and see grass and flowers and trees, say to yourself, " God has been here."

Are you thinking that I have forgotten about one place. In the desert, you say, there is no grass, nor flowers nor trees. Why is that ? I think I can tell you. You know, in your own garden, that you can't *play* over the place where the flowers are, so you have one patch where there are no flowers—the play-part. I believe that the desert is the play-part of the world that God has made for the animals, and there you will find them playing all day, and sometimes all night.

Hymn

God, who made the earth,
   The air, the sky, the sea,
Who gave the light its birth,
   Careth for me.

God, who made the grass,
   The flower, the fruit, the tree,
The day and night to pass,
   Careth for me.

II

GOD'S IMPERATIVES

" Come !—Listen !—Search ! "—Isaiah lv.

I mustn't make it sound too much like a grammar-lesson ; but suppose you were asked to parse all the verbs in this chapter. You will find that most of them are imperatives—come, buy, hearken, incline, seek, call. And imperatives are simply commands.

We have here a chapter of God's commands. Now the first and most important thing about a command is that it should be obeyed. There is a good rough-and-ready rule in the Army (though, of course, it has its exceptions, since these commands are man's, not God's) : Obey first, Ask afterwards. Even though the command looks strange, obey it ; and, when you have done that, ask questions if you want to. That rule once saved a man's life. We had just finished dinner in a dug-out in Palestine. This man rose up from his chair to go out on duty in the front-line trench, when his company commander suddenly cried out, " Sit down ! " And because he was a good soldier, he sat down at once with a flop in his chair. Then he wondered why. The company commander pointed to the wall. At the very place where his head had been a second before, there was a scorpion. It had been on the point of stinging him in the neck. If he had stopped even a second to ask why ? it would have had him.

Look at three of these commands of God. The

first, in verse one, is Come! Come to Church, God says. You have obeyed. You are here. Now, if you like, you can ask why? And the answer is easy. God cannot do anything for you unless you come to Him. Once upon a time there was a king who led a very lazy life. He had so many slaves that he never had to do anything for himself. He had one slave to carry his umbrella; one to put on his boots in the morning, and another to pull them off at night; one slave to comb his hair, and another to brush his teeth. One day he was on a journey through the desert. It was very hot and the king was thirsty. There was a well three miles away, but the king was too lazy to go to it. So he called one of his slaves and said, " Go to the well and take a good drink of water for me! " The slave went obediently. When he returned he said to the king, " Your majesty, I have taken a splendid drink of cool water for you. Does your majesty feel better? " But his majesty did not. " No," he growled, " no better. Go again and take a far bigger drink." The servant had nothing in which to carry the water, so he went again as he was told and took a bigger drink. The king, as you will imagine, felt no better. For twenty-four hours he suffered torments from thirst, and then in a fit of temper he said, " Dismiss that slave! Put him in a dungeon! Turn him loose in the desert! Tie him up with tent-ropes! And send another who can drink enough to quench my thirst."

Stupid, we say? Yet there are people who are just as foolish. Instead of coming to Church, they stay at home or go away for a day's holiday. " I'm too tired," they say, " to go to the well myself; I'll let someone else go for me; perhaps the children would like to go. It's so nice to see children in Church." But they can't expect God to do much for them if they won't come to Him. That is the first imperative —Come!

The second is in verse three, Listen! and the third in verse six, Search! Let us put them together in a story. Not very long ago, in South Africa, men were watching the ant-heaps. They could not understand why, when all the country was dry and parched, the ant-heaps were always cool and moist. Very carefully they began to examine one of the heaps, and they found by the side of the heap a passage like the shaft of a mine, going down and down into the earth— sixty-five feet down!—till it came to a stream, so far under the ground that the sun could not dry it up. It was always cool and fresh as ever; and there the ants were busy, day and night, running up and down, carrying water in their mouths and watering the soil of their heap. It is such an important task that all the ants are put on to it, not just a few picked for the job. Even those who come in from other fatigues set to work at once on this business of water-carrying. And how do they discover the water to begin with? They do it by obeying these two commands. First they *listen*. Then far away down below the surface they hear the lap and gurgle of the water. Then they *search*. They tunnel down and down in different directions towards the sound, till one of the scouts cries, " Here ! " The water is found.

There you have the reason for people coming to

Church : it is to listen for God and to search for Him. They need cool water to refresh them, and they know that Jesus can give them it.

And everyone is needed for this work. You are needed. You may not feel that you are hot and dusty and tired just now. But the older people are, and they need you to help them in finding God, to quench their thirst.

HYMN

Worship the Lord in the beauty of holiness !
  Bow down before Him, His glory proclaim ;
With gold of obedience and incense of lowliness,
  Kneel, and adore Him, the Lord is His name !

12

INTO THE LIGHT

" Shew forth the praises of Him who hath called you out of darkness into His marvellous light."—I PETER ii. 9.

IN *The Story of San Michele* you read of two boys, the one called Hans, the other Karl, who used to go to school together. On a dark winter morning you would hear them setting out from their village to walk through the deep snow to the school five miles away. Each carried his school-books tied together in a strap over his shoulder, and each carried in his hand a tallow candle. There was no gas in the school-room, but every boy brought his own candle with him. One by one they came in, stamping the snow off their boots and rubbing their hands to make them glow again. Then each would light his candle and set it on his own desk, till soon the whole room was ablaze with their shining. Each boy sat in a circle of light that enclosed his own desk. The master could call the roll quickly by noting the desks which were still dark. Sometimes an unlit desk meant that a boy had been snowed up and had had to turn back home again. Sometimes it meant that a boy was ill. Now and again, on a very cold morning, a boy would think, " I shan't be missed. One boy doesn't make much difference." But of course if every boy had thought the same and acted on it that school-room would be in darkness. Perhaps you think in that way sometimes about coming to Church to praise God and to worship. One, you say, will not be missed. Be sure, God misses your candle and the light you bring with you. God needs every one.

One day as the boys were making their way as usual by the light of the stars, they had a quarrel. It wasn't about very much : they hardly knew what it was about—you know the way that quarrels have—but they began to say bitter things of each other, until Hans cried out, " I'm going my own way ! " and he struck off the path over the frozen river and set out to reach the school by another way. It was a shorter road, but it wasn't a safe road : there were no posts to mark it, and they had often been warned not to go by that route until the Spring came round and melted the deep snow. He didn't care : he was going his own way. Karl plodded on and arrived at the school. He lighted the candle on his desk, but there was no light on the desk next to him. Hans was not there. Without saying anything, Karl blew out his candle and set off again. He made for the river where the other road began, and then struck off over the snow, following the footprints as well as he could. Two miles from the school he found Hans, lying asleep, exhausted and lost, the snow beginning to drift over him and conceal him. Karl dug him out. The candle was clutched tightly in his hand. He hoisted him on his shoulders and fought his way back to the school ; back into light and warmth and friendship. It was like the story of the one lost sheep, but in a way it was easier for them to understand, for they didn't know much about sheep in their country ; but they *did* know about getting lost in deep drifts and cruel blizzards. Ever afterwards when Hans read in the Bible about " the outer darkness," he thought of *out there* before Karl came. And when he heard this text, " Shew forth the praises of Him who hath called you out of the darkness into His marvellous light," he thought, for a long time, that it meant Karl, the boy who had saved his life.

Hans used to have a thick candle on his desk, for his parents were rich and could afford the best. Karl had the thinnest candle in the whole room, for his mother was poor.

Time went by and, though Karl had the smallest candle, he passed his exams. when some of the others failed. He had a tinier candle, but *he had more light in his brain*. He had more than that. He became a clever and famous doctor. Then one day the news reached him that a terrible epidemic of plague had broken out in a city in Italy. There were no doctors to look after the sick and the dying. Karl set off on the long journey from his own country to Italy, and there for weeks he worked day and night looking after the sick people when everyone else had left them to die. He had something better than " more light in his brain." He had a light in his soul that nothing could ever put out.

One dark night he came to the end. He had saved the lives of hundreds, but the plague caught him. God was calling him out of darkness into His marvellous light. He had forgotten, in his weakness, where he was. He thought he was going to school once again through the darkness and the deep snow.

But he had forgotten to bring his candle. And the old schoolmaster was saying to him, "Never mind, sonny, you won't need it this morning where you are going; there shall be no night there; and they need no candle, neither light of the sun; for the Lord God giveth them light : and they shall reign for ever and ever."

Hymn

Thou whose almighty word
Chaos and darkness heard,
   And took their flight,
Hear us, we humbly pray,
And, where the gospel day
Sheds not its glorious ray,
   Let there be light!

Thou who didst come to bring,
On Thy redeeming wing,
   Healing and sight,
Health to the sick in mind,
Sight to the inly blind,
O now to all mankind
   Let there be light!

13

BLACK MAGIC

I COULD see by the look in her eyes that she had something up her sleeve. (And I don't see why a dog should not have a sleeve : she has a coat, so why not a sleeve ? And it is about her coat that I want to tell you.)

"Dogs," she said, "are just like people. A very important point is that they should have the right colour of coat." I thought of Joseph's rare coat of many colours, yellow of the primrose, and blue of the hyacinth, and pink of the apple-blossom. But then you wouldn't expect to have a dog yellow, or blue, or even pink. And this one is none of these. She is just plain black.

At first I didn't want to speak about her coat because it was just plain black. It might suggest the black clouds that bring the rains and spoil your holidays, or the blackness of night in which the wild animals of the jungle creep out to hunt for their prey. But she saw at once what I was thinking, and she said, "But remember what the black clouds do for us. Where would the fields and the crops be to-day without the rain that the black clouds bring ? And even the black night is a lovely thing. Think," she said, "of the beautiful poem about it in Greek." And then, in case I didn't know any Greek, she translated it for me, kindly:

O Night that brings all things home, the sheep back to the fold and the child back to his mother.

" And then," she said, " you have the black diamonds, that are harder and stronger even than the others. (And I think we should give them a birthday-party, for it's just a hundred years since they were first discovered.) And besides, *you* should be quite happy about a black coat, because you often wear one yourself, and a black hat and a black umbrella as well : things that I never have ! "

She was so excited that I guessed she had something else up her sleeve. It was a text !

" Turn up the Song of Solomon," she said, " the first chapter and the fifth verse."

(She said it so naturally that you would have imagined she had been in Church twice every Sunday at least, instead of only that one morning when she crept in, a tiny black puppy, hid under a pew, and chewed. . . .)

" The first chapter and the fifth verse ! " she said, loudly and distinctly.

And there I read :

" I am black but comely."

" Comely ? " she asked. " Are you sure ? I thought it was ' black but comfy.' "

When I had explained what ' comely ' meant, she went on, " You see, it's quite easy to be black and still to be handsome. Black is the colour of the kitchen-range when it's well polished, and the colour of the shining pots, and the colour of shiny boots and shoes." And I thought too of some soldiers I once knew who were black but comely—grand men from the British West Indies who were coal-black in colour and yet were the kindest fellows and the best soldiers you could want.

When we speak about the British Empire it is interesting to count the people in it, by colour. I believe there are about 500 million altogether, and only one in every seven of these is white. The British Empire is not a white empire at all, but a coloured empire. And we are very proud of our black brothers. A small girl once asked her mother what became of chimney-sweeps in heaven. "Do they turn into *black* angels?"

No; it is just an accident whether we have a black face or a white one. We'll all be brothers in heaven and we are brothers here and now.

HYMN

Far round the world Thy children sing their song :
From East and West their voices sweetly blend,
Praising the Lord in whom young lives are strong,
Jesus our Guide, our Hero, and our Friend.

Thy sun-kissed children on earth's spreading plain,
Where Asia's rivers water all the land,
Sing, as they watch Thy fields of glowing grain,
Praise to the Lord who feeds them with His hand.

14

GELERT

" Dumb, and not able to speak."—LUKE i. 20.

WHEN I read these words, I often find myself thinking about dogs. " Dumb, and not able to speak "—that is just what dogs are. They have so much to say, and they can say it only by their eyes and their tails.

I am told that the number of dogs kept as pets in Britain alone is three and a half millions. If you put them all in a long row, nose to tail, the line would stretch from the south of England to the north of Scotland ; from Land's End to John o' Groats. And if they all barked at the same time they would be heard in Holland and Norway ; and even, if all the big ones were in the north of Scotland, at the North Pole itself. But a bark is not speech. They are all dumb, not able to speak—three and a half million dogs who cannot tell us what they need, and when they are feeling ill.

In a little village of Wales there is the grave of a famous dog. He was called Gelert, and the village is called after him, Beddgelert. This is his story :

He belonged to a great prince called Llewellyn. He was a greyhound, and a very valuable dog. He had been given to the prince as a present from the king. One day Llewellyn went out to battle against his enemies, and he left his little child under the charge of the faithful dog Gelert in the tent. At night, when the prince returned from battle, he found the tent thrown down and crumpled. The cradle was over-turned and the baby was nowhere to be seen. Then Gelert came out to meet him, and the dog's mouth was covered with blood. The prince cried out that the dog had turned traitor and had killed the child. In terrible anger, he drew his sword and stabbed Gelert. Then, suddenly, he heard a child's cry. Rushing to the cradle, he turned it over, and there was the baby safe and sound. By its side lay a huge wolf, torn and dead. He knew now that Gelert had saved the child by killing this fierce wolf. He ran to where the poor dog lay, and found him dying. Dumb and not able to speak, he had not known how to tell his master the truth. But, before he died, he looked up and licked the prince's hand, as much as to say, " It wasn't your fault, and I—I couldn't tell you of your mistake."

Llewellyn buried the dog with great honour, and built a magnificent grave for him. And there you can see his grave to this day. Thousands of people from all over the world come every year to this place, and whisper, " Poor Gelert ! " Above the grave there grows a weeping-ash.

It reminds us of a sadder story ; of One who was put to death through a tragic mistake ; One who came to save the lives of all the world but was not understood, and was put to death. That was the saddest part of it all. For it was not simply by wicked men that Jesus was put to death. It was just that they did not understand. We must be very careful not to make this terrible mistake.

Hymn

There is a green hill far away,
  Without a city wall,
Where the dear Lord was crucified
  Who died to save us all.

We may not know, we cannot tell
  What pains He had to bear ;
But we believe it was for us
  He hung and suffered there.

15

THE BROWNIES

" Do good and lend, hoping for nothing again ; and your reward shall be great."—LUKE vi. 35.

WE are proud to welcome our young guests in their brown, unobtrusive uniforms. "Unobtrusive," because their aim is to follow out these words of Jesus, "Do good and lend," and to do it so quietly that no one will know whose helping hand has been there. It is said that one of the happiest experiences of man is to "do good by stealth and be found out by accident"; but the Brownies try to keep the secret to themselves !

Their presence this morning reminds us of our responsibility towards the children of the congregation and of the parish. From their baptism onwards, from the day when their names are inscribed on our Cradle Roll, through Sunday Schools and Bible Classes, until they join with us as members of the Church at the Communion Table, they are our special care.

We record to-day our gratitude to this movement which assists us in fulfilling our duty towards them.

The movement has a splendid motto—"Lend a hand ! "—a little motto for little people, but one with a very large meaning. The Brownies have their special salute—with two fingers, to represent for them their twofold Promise. When a Brownie enrols, she promises—

To do her duty to God and the King.

To help other people every day, especially those at home.

These two promises are very comprehensive. They cover duty towards our faith and our native land; towards our homes and all whom we meet with. And the Brownies have their twofold Law:

> The Brownie gives in to the older people.
> The Brownie does not give in to herself.

There is discipline from without and discipline from within. That respect for age reminds us of the story from Athenian history. A large concourse had gathered for the public presentation of a play, when it was noticed that an old man was unable to find a place. The polished Athenian youths were discourteous enough to make a frolic of his embarrassment. But, when the man retreated towards the boxes appointed for the Spartans, that honest people, more virtuous than polished, rose up to a man and, with the greatest respect, led him to a place in their midst. The Athenians, touched with a sense of the Spartan virtue and their own inherent boorishness, gave a thunder of applause and the old man cried out, when it had died away, " The Athenians understand what is good, but the Lacedemonians practise it."

There is also a reciprocity in that respect. The old German schoolmaster, Trebonius, used always to appear before his boys with head uncovered. " Who can tell," he asked, " who may yet rise up among these youths ? " *His* reverence for the possibility in every child was abundantly justified; for even at that moment there was among the boys the young Martin Luther.

It is the custom of the Brownies, moreover, not generally to receive Christmas presents, but rather to bring them, so that they may be sent to children in less fortunate circumstances. They are learning the words of Jesus, "It is more blessed to give than to receive." The movement is tapping and conserving the inborn generosity of the child-mind.

And now a word to our guests themselves :

First, about your uniform. Like the soldiers, you wear brown so that you will not be easily seen as you go about your good deeds. You remember what Jesus said, "Do good and lend, hoping for nothing again." Goodness that has to be shouted about does not exist. You remember Little Jack Horner, sitting all by himself with his plum-cake and saying, "What a good boy am I!" No one else seems to have noticed it! As soon as you hear him say that, you suspect that he hasn't been good at all.

Your uniform, however, is enough to mark you out as Brownies. You have to live up to it. There was once some trouble in an American city, because the crossing-sweepers were not doing their job properly. They were growing lazy, and the crossings were not being well swept. Do you know what was done? They were all given white coats. Then everyone saw them. They couldn't be lazy without being seen. From that day the crossings were as neat as new pins. Of course, they shouldn't have needed that. You don't need to run for your uniform every time you want to do a good deed.

You are always Brownies, with your Promise and your Law.

Long ago in Scotland they used to speak about the Brownies. *They* weren't like you. They didn't belong to a Pack; they hadn't Brown Owls and Tawny Owls to look after them; they never came to Church. But, if there were some work to be done about the house, *they* came, people said; they finished it while it was still dark; and, before morning, they were gone and no one ever saw them. And I'm glad that your Promise begins at home. Where you have received so much love and happiness, you want to *lend a hand* in return.

The other day a teacher was telling her class about the Brownies and how you try to help at home. She said, " Now, if you saw your mother carrying a tray, and the door was shut, and her hands were so full that she couldn't open it, what would you do ? " With one voice the class cried, " Send for a Brownie ! "

Not quite right; but it shows what we think of you, and how we trust you to keep your promise.

It begins at home. But it doesn't end there. Let me tell you a story to show how far a helping hand can reach.

There was once a boy called Jan, who couldn't even help about the house, for he was a cripple. He lay all day on the flat roof of the house, getting the sunshine and playing with his toys. He hadn't many of them, but he had one special favourite, a book with coloured pictures telling of the life of Jesus. There was one picture of Jesus as a baby in His mother's arms; and pictures of the sick people being healed by Him; a picture of Him preaching to the crowds, and one of His crucifixion; of His rising again and of His going up to Heaven. And the last one showed Him sitting on a golden throne. They were beautiful pictures. They cheered him when he was in pain, and they helped him to say his prayers. Jan had only two friends. One was the doctor who came to see him. The other was a bird—a stork which used to nest every year on the roof near at hand. It had grown quite tame and would perch on the parapet and take bits of bread out of the boy's hand.

Jan often wished that he could do something big and useful and splendid with his life. He read about the men who travelled through strange countries. He liked Africa best, and he wished that he were strong enough to go out and help the black people there, and tell them about God. He used to ask the doctor about Africa. And one day, just as they were speaking about it, down flew the stork for his bread. The doctor smiled and said, "This old fellow could tell you more about Africa than anybody else, if he could speak." And he told Jan how the storks fly away from Europe in the autumn to spend the winter in a warm climate.

After that Jan took even more interest in his stork. He wished that it could speak and carry a message for him to Africa. Then a great idea came to him. He would write a letter and tie it to the stork's leg. Then when it settled on the black people's roofs, they would see the letter and read about Jesus. He spent many hours writing the message, and only when he had finished did he remember that the

African people would not be able to read his language.
What could he do? Another idea came to him.
He would send his book! They would understand
the pictures. It cost him a long struggle to give up
his favourite book; but he won. He made a bag
with a piece of waterproof stuff that his mother gave
him; put the letter in along with the book—just in
case they *could* read—and one day, when the stork
seemed to be fidgety and ready to fly away, he tied
it to the bird's leg. Not many days later, the stork
departed on its long journey.

Jan was lonely all winter, without his book. His
back was worse, too. And one day he overheard his
mother say that the only cure was a very expensive
treatment. Without that, she said, he would not live
more than six months. Jan began more than ever
to hope that the stork would deliver his message and
get back before he flew away himself.

One fine spring day there was a whirr of wings and
—there was the stork! Jan looked eagerly at his
leg. Yes; the bag was gone. But, in its place, was
a smaller bag, a tiny pouch of rough leather. An
answer! Jan's fingers trembled so much with excitement that he could scarcely unknot the cord. And
then—out fell three sparkling jewels, a red, a green,
and a white. At the bottom of the bag a tiny roll of
paper—a letter, and in Jan's own language. It was
written by a missionary. It told how he came one
day to a village where the men had always refused to
listen to his preaching; where they were all very
fierce and very cruel. But this day they welcomed
him, and asked him to tell them about the great white

God who came to earth as a child, and healed the sick, and went up to heaven, and sits on a golden throne, and now uses storks as His messengers. The missionary was puzzled till he saw the book and the letter. The king's little son had found them tied to the leg of his own tame stork ! This had given the missionary his opportunity. He had talked to them about Jesus, and they wanted now to be baptised and to become Christians. They asked him to write this letter, and the king took from his treasury these three jewels as a remembrance for their friend across the seas.

That was a fine example of your motto in action— " Lend a hand ! "

Jesus says, " And your reward shall be great." You can guess what happened in the case of Jan. When the doctor called next day he heard all about the exciting happenings. He carried away the jewels to an expert and found that they were worth £2,000 —more than enough to pay for the expensive cure.

To-day Jan is a grown man with straight back and strong arms. He writes wonderful books and does great good in the world. But he always says that the finest thing he ever did in his life was to send his book of pictures—and he missed it !—to win the hearts of an African tribe.

HYMN

Dear Master, what can children do ?
    The angels came from heaven above
To comfort Thee ; may children too
    Give Thee their love ?

No more as on that night of shame,
   Art Thou in dark Gethsemane,
Where worshipping, an angel came
   To strengthen Thee.

But Thou hast taught us that Thou art
   Still present in the crowded street,
In every lonely, suffering heart
   That there we meet :

And not one simple, loving deed,
   That lessens gloom, or lightens pain,
Or answers some unspoken need,
   Is done in vain.

16

CROAKING AND PRAISING

*" I waited patiently for the Lord ; and He inclined unto me, and heard
my cry. He brought me up also out of an horrible pit, out of the
miry clay, and set my feet upon a rock, and established my goings.
And He hath put a new song in my mouth, even praise unto our God."*
—Psalm xl. 1–3.

You have been keeping your eyes wide open for the
signs of Spring—for nests and eggs, for the first
swallows and the first cuckoo. If you looked into
some of the ditches along the meadowside perhaps
you saw a very interesting bit of the Spring—the
frogs' nurseries. It is good to see the first tadpoles
beginning to launch out in the world, giving their
tails a few practice swishes before they set off for
their first swim.

There is a story about the Frogs. You know how
they go to sleep in the winter, all huddled together
in the mud at the bottom of a pond. One day, in the
middle of winter, they wakened up, and stretched
themselves a little before rolling over on the other
side. And they made a terrible discovery. Frost had
come in the night, and the pond was frozen over.
For us the ice means fun ; but to the Frogs it meant,
they imagined, that they were prisoners for ever.
There seemed to be no escape. Hemmed in above
and below, they thought the end had come. And,
they said, if ever we are set free again—it's not likely—
but if ever we are, we won't croak any more in that
old, gruff fashion, as if we were sulky or bad-tempered;

we'll sing; we'll sing like nightingales! Yes, like nightingales!

Of course, they *were* set free. The Spring came. It always does come. God never fails. We remember how He came to set Jesus free from the grave, to rise again on Easter morning into the sunlight. The Spring came round, and the ice melted, and the Frogs came out of their pond, and began to sing their joy. But it was the same old croak. Perhaps they were doing their best. If they were really thankful and really trying to say Thanks, I am sure that God heard their praises and liked the croak just as much as if it had been a nightingale's song.

I dare say that you are often in a hole like the frogs, and you say, If ever I get out of this trouble I'll be so thankful that I'll never get into trouble again. God has forgiven us so often. We shall praise Him.

Is it the same old croak? Or is it the best we can do? Do we really try our best to praise God like the nightingales?

HYMN

He took me from a fearful pit,
    And from the miry clay,
And on a rock He set my feet,
    Establishing my way.

He put a new song in my mouth,
    Our God to magnify:
Many shall see it and shall fear,
    And on the Lord rely.

17

CHRIST IS RISEN!

(AN EASTER STORY)

ONCE upon a time there was an old man who had a strange adventure. It was growing dark in the little village, and, because it was April, the setting sun drew a lovely mist out of the ground, so that the trees were all hidden. Only the stars could be seen now, and the outline of the tiny church against the sky.

If you had been passing that night you would have heard the creaking of the stairs as the old man climbed up into the belfry, and you would have seen his lantern shining out like a star hung in the heavens. He was going up into the tower to ring the bells for Easter morning.

He was a *very* old man and he had buried many friends during his long life. As he rested against the balusters, he looked down into the cemetery and saw their graves in the dim light, with their little crosses standing over them.

He did not need any watch to tell him when it was time to ring the bells, for he knew all the stars, and he had rung the peals so often to bring in Easter morning.

At last it was time, and he grasped the familiar ropes. In a moment the night echoed with the musical notes, and the people began to come out of their homes and across the grass to the Church. The bells stopped, and the service began. The old man was too feeble to go down the stairs again, but he could watch the service through a window from where he was, up in the belfry-tower. In one of the pews he saw his wife kneeling, and he rubbed his eyes, for she had been buried many years ago in the cemetery below. And now she looked so radiant and so happy. He wondered why he had been sad for her these many years. And beside her he saw their gallant son, who had not been buried in the cemetery, for he had gone to the wars and had never come back. He was so proud to see him again that he did not notice when the service was over, and he did not hear the people coming out of Church till they called up to him, " Hullo, there ; are you asleep ? " They were waiting for him to ring the bells again to tell the country-side that it was Easter morning. With a start he called his mind back and took the friendly ropes again. Then he rang so wonderfully that the people below cried out that the bells had never rung so joyously before. It seemed as if the old man's happy heart had passed into their tones, while all the bells called together over the wide plains, " Christ is risen ! Christ is risen ! " The old belfry seemed to rock with the joy of it, " Christ is risen ! " On and on they rang, and still the people whispered, " Never has he rung so well before." Then there came an uncertain sound from the largest bell, and quite suddenly it stopped. The smaller ones rang out an unfinished tone, and then the music died away on the quivering air. The old bell-ringer sank back exhausted on the bench, and the last tears of joy slipped down his cheeks. When they found him, he had rung his final peal.

It was no wonder that he looked so happy as he lay there, for Jesus had stood beside him as he rang, " Christ is risen ! " It was true. And now the old bell-ringer had risen with Him. He was laughing and talking with his wife and with his gallant son, and he wondered again why he had ever been sad.

Hymn

" Christ the Lord is risen to-day,"
Sons of men and angels say :
Raise your joys and triumphs high :
Sing, ye heavens, and earth reply.

Lives again our glorious King ;
Where, O death, is now thy sting ?
Once He died our souls to save :
Where thy victory, O grave ?

18

HERALDS OF DANGER

*"O all ye fowls of the air, bless ye the Lord :
Praise Him and magnify Him for ever."*—DANIEL iii. 80
(Greek version).

WE can hear the birds praising and blessing the Lord. Morning and night they are singing to Him. What is it that they are thanking Him for ?

The birds have a great deal for which to be thankful. We know of the wonderful feats performed by homing-pigeons ; how they used to fly home to this country from as far away as Rennes, in Brittany, across the sea and through storms, right back to their own lofts. Who is it who guides them home ? It is God ; for He has given them that instinct by which they can find their way over hundreds of miles—an instinct which has not been given to us. No wonder the birds praise God for looking after them like this. The Father in Heaven, Jesus tells us, cares for every sparrow.

There is another kind of bird which flies in a wonderful way over the sea—the stormy petrel. It can fly about from morning to night without tiring. It has a very strong wing and a very stout heart. Sometimes it comes so close to the water that it seems to be walking on the waves, and that is how it got its name. Petrel is just *Petrello*, and that is Italian for 'Little Peter.' You remember how Peter walked on the water, but he was afraid and he began to sink. This little bird has more faith than Peter.

There is another name for this bird. Sailors call the petrels "Mother Carey's Chickens." That seems like a nickname, but it too comes from the New Testament. Mother Carey is from two Latin words, *Mater Cara*, or Mother Dear. Hundreds of years ago the sailors, being Roman Catholics, worshipped Mary the Mother of Jesus. They called her Dear Mother, or *Mater Cara*, or Mother Carey; and they thought that these birds, the petrels, were her messengers. The petrels, you know, feed on small fish which they snatch from the waves; and they get most of them when the weather is stormy. Thus you find them in the greatest numbers flying over the water when there is a storm approaching. The sailors used to notice this, and to say that Mary was sending her messengers to warn them. So 'Mother Carey's Chickens' means simply 'messengers of Mary'; God's heralds of danger.

And God does send messengers to tell us too about coming danger. One of them is your conscience, that voice which says to you, 'Don't do that: it is wrong; you are in danger: beware.' And He sends also teachers and parents, wise people who have seen these same dangers before, and can warn you about them.

The wise sailor looks out for all these warnings and obeys them; so that he escapes disaster. The wise person does the same. You will not run into danger if you listen always to the voices of God.

HYMN

O let the earth bless the Lord :
Yea, let it praise Him and magnify Him for ever.

O all ye green things upon the earth, bless ye the Lord :
Praise Him and magnify Him for ever.

O ye seas and floods, bless ye the Lord :
Praise Him and magnify Him for ever.

O all ye fowls of the air, bless ye the Lord :
Praise Him and magnify Him for ever.

O ye children of men, bless ye the Lord :
Praise Him and magnify Him for ever.

19

THE SILLY TIGER

" There were they in great fear where no fear was."—PSALM liii. 5.

IT is not very often that you catch a tiger being afraid, but once it happened in a comical way. An Indian juggler—who went about the country making money by conjuring-tricks—was going out for a walk one fine evening when his day's work was over. He was just crossing a beautiful plain when, five or six hundred yards away, he spied a tiger sharpening its teeth. Before he could hide, the tiger had spied him too and began bounding towards him at top speed. The Indian had no gun with him and the only chance of escape lay in making for the nearest tree. He turned and ran as fast as his trembling legs would carry him ; but it wasn't fast enough : the tiger was gaining on him with every bound. It would have him before he could reach safety. Then he had a brilliant idea. Ahead of him was a small ridge, and he knew that for a few seconds, no more, he would be out of sight while he was running down the other side. Now was his only chance. As soon as he was out of sight, he stopped, and began to do one of the tricks with which he used to amuse the people of the villages. He spread his legs out as far as he could, curled down his head between his knees so that he was looking backwards through his legs, and he stretched out his arms above him like the sails of a windmill. In a few seconds the tiger appeared. At once the man let out a blood-curdling yell such as no respectable tiger had ever heard before. And the sails of the windmill began to go round and round and round as if a violent storm had begun to blow.

The tiger sprang aside. " Whatever is this ? " he said to himself. For there stood a fierce star-shaped monster huge against the sky. Its terrible head was in the very middle of its body and its mouth was actually above its glaring eyes ! Its great arms were spinning round and round and round ready to seize its enemy. Already it must have eaten the man he was chasing, for there was no sign of him anywhere. The tiger would not stay to think it over. He turned tail and ran and ran till he lost himself in the jungle. He was beaten by the unknown. He was afraid where no fear was.

If you had to play the part of one of these, I think you would rather be the juggler—at least when it was all safely over. It would be a wonderful story to tell ! But suppose for a moment you are the tiger. How you would be teased when at last you found your way home ! How the other tigers would laugh at you when they heard the truth ! Beaten by a man because he put his head between his legs !

A tiger's job in life is to catch men and eat them. It's not much of a job, but the tiger doesn't know any better : it's the only employment he can find. And this one failed in his job because he was afraid of the unknown.

I think there are some tigers among ourselves. We don't call them that, or they would feel hurt. We call them ' superstitious people.' They tell you that something dreadful will happen to you if you spill the salt, or if you set out on a journey on a Friday. They are afraid where no fear is. I wonder what they think about God, if they imagine that He would make some terrible thing happen to us, because we spill the salt, or go on a journey on a Friday? You would understand, perhaps, that people who had never heard about God might be afraid like that. It may be natural for them to fear the unknown, for they have never heard of Jesus and the God of Love whom He called 'Father.' But we have heard, and, if we are afraid of little things like spilling the salt and setting out on a journey on a Friday, we are just silly tigers.

We have no need to be afraid at all, for Jesus loves us.

Hymn

Light of the world, undimming and unsetting !
    O shine each mist away ;
Banish the fear, the falsehood, and the fretting ;
    Be our unchanging Day.

20

MR. FEARING

" They were afraid, and came."—ISAIAH xli. 5.

SOME of us are afraid when we have to go to the
dentist. One dentist told me how he once had a
famous lawyer in his chair, and, when the dentist
came back into the room after getting an instru-
ment, the chair was empty. The man had suddenly
taken fright and run away. That was a man who
was afraid and came; then was more afraid and—
went! I know of another man, now a great poet,
who had to go to the dentist also. He got as far as
the door and then his courage failed him, and he
couldn't bring himself to ring the bell. He had to
stop someone who was passing at the time and say,
" Would you mind please ringing this bell for me ? "
That was a man who was afraid and yet—*came, and
stayed*.

Now, it is natural to be afraid of the dentist. But
I have heard of people who are afraid of coming to
Church! Many, many years ago, our forefathers
used to meet on the hillside to worship God, because
they were not allowed to go into Church. And some
of them, I feel sure, were a little afraid. For the
soldiers were sent to arrest them and to have them,
perhaps, put to death. So the people had to post
sentries to tell them when the soldiers were approaching. Some, I am sure, were afraid, and yet that did
not keep them away. They were afraid, but they came.

I have heard too of a man who is afraid even to-day, and even in our own free and happy land, to go to Church. Not because of soldiers, but because—what do you think?—because people may laugh at him! His friends say to him, "Why are you so goody-goody as to go to Church? Come along with us for a game of tennis on Sunday morning." And he is so afraid of them that he goes. When I heard that, I thought about a man in Africa who had reason to be afraid of going to Church. When he became a Christian, his family were very angry. They caught him and beat him almost to death, and dared him to go to Church again. But next Sunday there he was again as brave as ever. He may have been afraid in his heart, but he came.

That is the story of a white coward and a black hero.

Of course, you are not afraid to come to Church. No one will send soldiers to arrest you to-day; no one will beat you for going. But I think we should be very proud of our forefathers who used to come even at the risk of their lives; and of men and women in many parts of the world to-day who take enormous risks in order to worship God. It is such people who have made it possible for us to come so safely and so happily to Church to-day. Is it not sad to think that there are still big people who are afraid to come to Church—afraid that others will laugh at them? I want you to show them the way. Every Sunday morning, I should like to see you flocking into Church. Then those who are afraid to come will say, "Why, that is where I should be too."

74

Hymn

All people that on earth do dwell,
　　Sing to the Lord with cheerful voice;
Him serve with fear, His praise forth tell;
　　Come ye before Him, and rejoice.

O enter then His gates with praise,
　　Approach with joy His courts unto;
Praise, laud, and bless His name always,
　　For it is seemly so to do.

21

LIGHTS AND SHADOWS

" When His candle shined upon my head, and when by His light I walked through darkness."—JOB xxix. 3.

NOWADAYS we are very fond of light—when we can get it. We are so fond of it that, to make up for the black-out hours, we are getting up two hours earlier in the morning, so that in order to be in good time for school at nine we are rising about five o'clock (and calling it ' seven ').

How did they manage in the days before gas light and electric light were invented? Suppose we cast back our minds to the days of the very distant past. In the museums we can learn to-day something of their manner of life. We can see, for example, mummies from Egypt which are very ancient. If you look closely at some of these mummies, you will find a small hole in the foot. Once upon a time a tiny lamp was fixed in the hole. They tried to make the mummies as life-like as possible, and this lamp helped. There were no street-lamps in those days. You might be stepping into a hole or a puddle without knowing it ; so, when they went out at night, men fastened a small lamp to their feet. They carried their own street-lighting about with them ! These lamps were even more valuable if men had to go through the jungle or through the desert, where snakes might be lying hidden in the darkness right on the path.

Thy Word, says the Bible, " God's Word is a lamp unto my feet." Wherever there is darkness and trouble and danger lying in wait for us, the Bible will give the light that will see us through. " By His light I walked through darkness."

There is often danger at our feet. But there may also be danger at the head. Some people imagine that they can get along very well without the Bible. They are so clever, they fancy, they have such good heads, that they have no need of it. They will push on and get what they want for themselves and never mind anything else. We say that they are ' wrapped up in themselves.' (What a queer bundle !) We must never be that. " *The man who is wrapped up in himself makes a very small parcel.*"

There is a grand example of the right way to be found in a famous man, Michael Angelo, the painter and sculptor. When he was working on a picture or on a statue, he always wore, it is said, a lighted candle fastened to the peak of his cap (not unlike the miner's lamp which we see sometimes). When they asked him, Why ? he said, " No shadow of myself must fall on the work." And that was true in every way of all his work. That is why he is so great. He thought always of his work and never of himself.

Job wanted to get back to the time when God's candle shined upon his head and by His light he walked through darkness. But there is one greater example. Jesus pleased not Himself, but gave Himself for us all.

F 77

Hymn

Thou did'st leave Thy throne
And Thy kingly crown.
When Thou camest to earth for me;
But in Bethlehem's home
Was there found no room
For Thy holy nativity :
   O come to my heart, Lord Jesus ;
   There is room in my heart for Thee.

Heaven's arches rang
When the angels sang,
Proclaiming Thy royal degree ;
But of lowly birth
Cam'st Thou, Lord, on earth,
And in great humility :
   O come to my heart, Lord Jesus ;
   There is room in my heart for Thee.

22

THE GARDEN PLOT

" Inasmuch."—MATTHEW xxv. 40.

IN the West of Africa there is a famous college. We have reason to be proud of it. All the students are black boys and the youngest are the best of all. Some of them are only three and a half.

A friend of mine who was a professor there told me a story about it. He used to teach the boys how to grow plants and shrubs and vegetables and flowers ; and, to encourage them, he offered a prize for the best garden. There was one small boy who was only seven, but he had entered for the competition for boys under ten, and he was determined to win. He planted rows and rows of the finest seeds. He was very careful of them. I think he dug them up only twice to see how they were getting on ; and he always planted more after that ; and, when his favourite turkey broke loose and scratched up the seeds, he began all over again with great patience. The time came round, and he thought he had certainly the best rows. He would get the prize. And then—then he fell ill ; so ill that he could do nothing in the garden. He lay in bed, thinking of the flowers withering for want of water, and the weeds growing all over the plots, and the turkeys running turkey-races up and down his vegetables. Through the window he could see the other boys passing back and forward every morning and evening. He thought they would be pointing at his wilting flowers. He heard them laughing and chattering among themselves, and he felt sure they were laughing at the weeds which were covering his plots.

The prize-day came. When he wakened in the morning, he thought of his ruined garden, and of the prize he had lost, and he brushed away a tear or two ; for he was only seven. That day the doctor allowed him to go out for the first time. He wandered along sadly to his garden to see how bad it was. And what do you think he saw ? Instead of withered flowers, he saw flowers more beautiful and stately than ever. Instead of weeds, he saw a garden perfectly trimmed and kept. Even the turkeys seemed to be drawn up on parade, standing at attention and dressing by the right. Now he knew what the other boys had been doing these mornings and evenings. They had been weeding and trimming and digging and watering in *his* garden. He was ill, they said, and they weren't going to let him lose the prize because of a little thing like that. And there, at the top of his garden, he saw the red card which said

FIRST PRIZE

" Inasmuch," Jesus says, " as ye have done it unto the least of these little ones—even to a little black boy of seven, ill in bed—ye have done it unto Me."

Hymn
O what can little hands do
    To please the King of heaven ?
The little hands some work may try,
To help the poor in misery :
    Such grace to mine be given.

23

THE PICNIC

THIS is the story of a strange picnic. The schools were on holiday. One morning a small boy wakened up and said to himself, " I wonder if Mother would let me go a picnic to-day ? " He was a lonely little chap, for he had no brothers or sisters, and he was too small to play with the big boys in the village. At breakfast he asked his mother. " You see," he said ; " I want to get some tadpoles, and I know where there are some lovely flowers you would like."

So he was allowed to go, but only for half a day. He was to set off after dinner and be home for supper, and his mother baked him some delicious scones and wrapped them up for him.

Off he went, feeling very proud and important about his first picnic all alone. When he got away out into the country, he thought he would pretend that he was an explorer, in a wild land where no one else had ever been. He pretended that he was three thousand miles from home, and that he had nothing else to eat for a month but his scones. He would try how long he could make them last out. So, at tea-time, he ate only one, and had still five left.

About six o'clock, from the top of a hill, he saw a great crowd in the valley beyond. At first he thought that he had really come into a foreign land, and that this was an army of fierce barbarians coming out to take him prisoner, and then, when he saw that the people were quite quiet, he decided that it must be a Sunday School picnic, for there were a number of children too. He went nearer and hung about on the edge of the crowd to see what it was all about. And he heard someone say, " They've forgotten all about their food." That gave him a shock. A Sunday School picnic and no tea ! What a terrible mistake ! He was glad to feel his scones safe in his pocket, and glad after all that he wasn't an explorer, but that he would be back home in an hour or two for his warm supper.

Then he saw a wee chap, far smaller even than himself, burst out crying, because he was so hungry ; and he thought to himself, " I wonder if I could hold out till I get home without food ? It's a long way on an empty stomach, but I believe I could do it." And, very shyly, he went up to one of the men who seemed to be one of the Sunday School teachers and said, " I've got some scones somewhere. Would you give them to that wee hungry boy ? I can hold out. I'm used to exploring."

Then the strange thing happened. There came forward another man, with a happy face, and the kindest smile the boy had ever seen. He took the scones, saying, " Thank you," and held them in his hands while he asked a blessing and the boy took off his cap. Then the man took the boy's hand, and somehow the boy felt strangely happy. He wasn't hungry any longer and he felt tremendously *safe* because of that strong hand in his. (He didn't know why, but I expect you have guessed. The man was Jesus.) And the boy saw *his* scones being given to all the people. How it happened he never could tell, but they seemed to grow as they went along, till all that great crowd of people had picnicked on his five scones. And, lastly, Jesus gave him his share, and never before had his mother's scones tasted so fine.

When he arrived home for supper, he couldn't explain to his mother *how* it had happened, but always after that he was quite sure that nothing was impossible for this new friend called Jesus.

HYMN

I've found a Friend; O such a Friend!
   He loved me ere I knew Him;
He drew me with the cords of love,
   And thus He bound me to Him;
And round my heart still closely twine
   Those ties which nought can sever;
For I am His, and He is mine,
   For ever and for ever.

24

THE ACORN-ELEPHANT

" I will praise Thee, for I am fearfully and wonderfully made."
—PSALM cxxxix. 14.

THERE is one kind of story we are all fond of reading —the story of great triumphs of Engineering. We like to hear how famous bridges were built, and bicycles and aeroplanes invented, and submarines made. Sometimes we try to make models of these things ourselves.

This is the story of the ' Acorn-Elephant.' He is not a full-sized elephant like the one you see in the circus (which unhappily war has taken away from us for a little), but an elephant which is only the size of a beetle. A famous man was once watching the insects in the woods around his home, when he saw a curious one. It was called an ' elephant,' because it carries a long nose—as long as its whole body—like an elephant's trunk. The nose is so big that the insect has to carry it straight and stiff out in front of it. (It would be awkward, I have no doubt, when the air-raid warden came to fit it for a gas-mask.) The scientist watched to see what use would be made of this ' trunk.' Then he discovered its purpose. It is used for piercing a hole in an acorn, in which to lay an egg. He watched it at work. It took up a stance on the slippery side of an acorn. (You might expect it to fall off, but God has prepared against this too. He has given it little sticky sandals, so that it can even climb up a sheet of glass without slipping.) Then it begins its great engineering feat. Its long nose turns out to be a beautiful drill. It pushes it into the acorn. Then it walks round in a half-circle to the right, and then back again in a half-circle to the left. Back and forwards it goes, till it has pierced right down to the cup of the acorn. Then it puts its egg at the very bottom of the long shaft, and, in time, a young ' elephant ' is hatched out.

When the man saw this wonderful shaft being sunk, he asked himself two questions. The first was this, " Why does it put the egg right at the bottom of the shaft ? Would it not be easier to place it just beneath the surface ? " And this is the answer which he soon discovered. It puts it at the bottom of the shaft because the young beetle will find the best food there when it comes out. It will need very soft food, like all children. And the softest food is right at the foot. In the cup of the acorn is some fine cottony stuff, just the thing for babies. And the cottony stuff is steeped in a juice called ' tannin.' Tannin is the juice which we have in tea, so that the mother puts the egg where the young beetle will have breakfast waiting for it whenever it comes out—plenty of soft bread and a cup of tea.

The other question was, " Why does the mother not bore down by the shortest way ? " It might begin at the cup and bore straight in by the quickest route. The answer once again is—food. When the small beetle has finished its bread and its cup of tea, it is not yet strong enough to tackle the hard stuff of the acorn. But, in the long tunnel which the mother has made, it finds plenty of crumbs, broken off in the boring. These crumbs last it until it is strong enough to tackle the hard meat of the acorn itself.

There is one other wonderful and surprising thing about this engineering feat. Very often the mother bored the whole tunnel and then went off without leaving any egg in the acorn. Why? It seemed a waste of labour. This is the answer. She had found that the food in this cup was not good enough for her young beetle. When the nurse is giving some broth to the child, she tastes it first herself, to make sure it is all right. The acorn-elephant does the same; and, if she finds that the food is of poor quality, she goes elsewhere.

When we read that story, we realise that the world round about us is like a big Bible. Every page tells how wonderful God is. He has made these amazingly clever engineers. And He has made us with all our marvellous powers. We can walk and run; we can see and hear; we can talk; we can build bridges and houses and aeroplanes. We are fearfully and wonderfully made. We will praise Him.

HYMN

There is a book, who runs may read,
　　Which heavenly truth imparts,
And all the lore its scholars need,
　　Pure eyes and Christian hearts.

The works of God above, below,
　　Within us and around,
Are pages in that book, to show
　　How God Himself is found.

THE ACORN-ELEPHANT

Thou who hast given me eyes to see
 And love this sight so fair,
Give me a heart to find out Thee,
 And read Thee everywhere.

25

IRON OUT OF THE SKY

" Every good gift and every perfect gift is from above, and cometh down from the Father."—JAMES i. 17.

THIS is a text which we remember specially at the time of Harvest Thanksgiving ; but it is good also for any time of the year and any time of our life.   Wherever we go, we find God sending the gifts which are necessary for life.   Suppose we go, for example, to the Polar regions, where there are no harvest-fields. What do we find ?   In the land where the Eskimos live, there are no metals : no iron, no copper, no tin. Indeed, mines would be of little use, for in that climate they could not be worked.   But the Eskimos needed iron, for their spears in hunting and their hooks in fishing.   And the Father gave them what they needed, in two ways.

First from the sea.   Planks and pieces of wood with nails in them used to come floating in from the ocean, and from these they took out the nails and made them into spear-points and hooks.   But, more than a century ago, an explorer noticed that they had tiny knives of a different kind of iron.   Little bits of iron, about the size of a sixpence, were fastened in wooden grooves in a piece of stick.   He asked them where they got the metal and they answered, strangely, that they had broken it off from pieces of a mountain far away.

It seemed a queer tale, the fable of an iron moun-

tain; but explorers set themselves to find if there
was any truth in the story. And one day, sure enough,
they discovered the iron mountain. As a matter of
fact, it was not a mountain, but three masses of metal.
There was one small one, which was called 'The
Dog,' because it was just about the size of a large
dog. The next was called 'The Man,' but it
weighed about three tons. And the third they named
'The Giant': it weighed 100 tons.

Where do you think they came from? They came
straight from Heaven! They were what we call
meteorites—masses of metal that had fallen from the
sky.

Once upon a time they had gone round and round
in the sky, like tiny planets; till one day they were
caught by the attraction of our planet; caught as if in
a net; and they fell down on the earth. What alarm
they must have caused if there were any people near
when they landed. Not so very long ago, such a
mass of metal fell in India; and a poor Indian peasant
thought that his end had come. He could not tell
very exactly what had happened. He was so frightened that he believed the meteor had chased him for
two hours through the jungle before it finally crashed
to the earth.

That was an exciting way for the metal to come to
the Eskimos. And yet the things we need come in
just as exciting a fashion. Nothing could be more
wonderful than the way in which the corn comes
through the ground in the Spring, and grows up
and up till it is ready to be turned into the bread
we eat.

Every good and every perfect gift comes from above ; comes from the Father in Heaven.

HYMN

Lord of all being, throned afar,
Thy glory flames from sun and star ;
Centre and soul of every sphere,
Yet to each loving heart how near.

Grant us Thy truth to make us free,
And kindling hearts that burn for Thee,
Till all Thy living altars claim
One holy light, one heavenly flame.

26

THE GUESTS OF GOD

" When thou makest a feast, call the poor, the maimed, the lame, the blind."—LUKE xiv. 13.

WHEN Jesus gives a feast, the first invitations go out to the poor, the crippled, the blind. Let me tell you of a little happening I watched for a month or two in one of our Scottish cities. In a house in the suburbs there are about twenty children ; a big family ; and all of them are maimed or lame. They had a Sunday School all to themselves in the drawing-room, but one day the matron heard them say, " Wouldn't it be grand if we could go to Church like the other children, instead of being cooped up here every Sunday morning."

The matron told some friends what she had heard, and the friends said, " Why not ? " They put their heads together and this was the result. Next Sunday morning at half-past ten, the nurses had all the children dressed and ready to go out. When they asked in surprise, " Where are we going ? " the nurses only replied, " Wait and see." At a quarter to eleven a number of motor-cars drew up at the door, and five children were lifted into each car. They were going to Church ! What about those who couldn't walk even a step ? They were remembered too. A tall, strong young man walked in at the front door. (You know him. You have seen his photograph in the newspapers and heard his name on the radio.) The day before he had been playing for Scotland in a famous Rugby match. He was so good at carrying a Rugger ball that they thought he would certainly be good at carrying lame children. Some of the children, in fact, pretended to be a great deal worse than they were, for the honour of being carried to Church by a Rugby internationalist. (And he promised faithfully not to do any drop kicks on the way.)

Always they tried to be specially well dressed for their visit to Church. One Sunday a small boy called John S. was wearing a fine pair of white gloves. At least you would think they were white gloves until you looked closely, and then you would see that, by mistake, in his hurry and excitement that morning, he had taken a pair of white socks instead of his gloves. Nevertheless he wore them manfully all the time, although it is a little difficult to turn over the pages of the hymn-book when there are no fingers in your gloves.

But the most interesting person in that house was a girl called Joan. Joan was not only lame : she was also blind. The doctors could do nothing for her. They could not even keep her in the children's hospital, since the beds were all needed for those who had a chance of getting better, and Joan, they said, had none. So she was sent to the Infirmary and put in a ward where there were only old people and no other children to talk to or to play with. Then her Sunday School teacher made a plan. She was taking all the other lame children in the summer for a fortnight in camp. They wouldn't be able to play many camp-games, being so lame, but they could have good fun, watching the birds and the rabbits, and lying on their beds round the camp-fire at night. Could Joan not come too? They would look well after her. The doctor considered it for a moment or two and then said, "Yes; certainly. Poor Joan, she can't ever get better, but it will do her no harm, and it will make her a bit happier." So Joan went to camp and lay in her pram all day in the sunshine.

And then the marvellous thing began to happen. She had been only a week there, getting fine fresh milk and eggs, and breathing in the pure air, when her cheeks commenced to turn pink and rosy and she found that she could move, ever so little, a foot which she had not moved for five years. Then one day, towards the end of the second week in camp, she gave a sudden cry of delight, "I can see! I can see!"

It was perfectly true. How it happened I cannot tell you. The doctors were puzzled. I only know that there had been much kindness and love shown to her during those two weeks, and kindness and love can do marvellous things. For Jesus is behind them.

HYMN

From Thee all skill and science flow,
    All pity, care, and love,
All calm and courage, faith and hope,
    O pour them from above.

And hasten, Lord, that perfect day
    When pain and death shall cease,
And Thy just rule shall fill the earth
    With health, and light, and peace.

27

"NEVER FEARED THE FACE OF MAN"

" The Lord is my helper : I will not fear what man shall do unto me."
—HEBREWS xiii. 6.

IN the heart of Edinburgh a man is buried of whom a nobleman said, as he looked down into the open grave, " There lies one who never feared the face of man."

The first time we meet this fearless man, he is walking in front of a great crowd, carrying a two-handed sword. They have been to hear George Wishart preaching, and everyone knows that men are trying to kill Wishart. Not long ago a priest of the Roman Catholic Church had tried to stab him, and in a very short time he will be burned to ashes in the city of St. Andrews. Many others have been burned already, but this does not frighten John Knox, the man with the two-handed sword. His friend Wishart says to him, " Return to your bairns, and God bless you. One is sufficient for a sacrifice." But Knox does not hear. He has his duty to do.

When next we see him, Knox has been taken prisoner and has been sent as a slave to a French galley. Chained to the oars, he has no shelter from rain or wind. On his shoulders are long purple scars where the whip of the slave-driver has bitten. One dies and then another, and are thrown into the sea. There is a painted image on board which the Roman Catholics try to make Knox worship ; but not even now is Knox afraid. He takes the image and throws it into the sea. There, he says, if it is as powerful as you think, it will swim to shore !

Try as they would, no one could make Knox afraid. Instead, the priests became desperately afraid of him. One of the bishops was so alarmed at the man and at his preaching that he hired twelve guns, called ' culverins,' and gave orders that, if Knox appeared, they were all to open fire on him at once. It seems a lot of guns for sniping at one man, but they didn't succeed in keeping Knox away. He simply took out his diary and wrote in it a little joke about the bishop. By order of the bishop, he wrote, " ye shall gar John Knox be saluted with a dosane of culveringis, quereof the most parte should lyght upoun his nose ! " and in the margin he wrote, " The Bishope his Goode Minde toward Johne Knox."

" One who never feared the face of man." We wonder how he was able to keep so calm. The answer is in the text :

" *The Lord* is my helper ; I will not fear what *man* shall do unto me."

HYMN

God is my strong salvation ;
    What foe have I to fear ?
In darkness and temptation
    My light, my help is near.

Though hosts encamp around me,
    Firm to the fight I stand ;
What terror can confound me,
    With God at my right hand ?

28

FLOWER SERVICE

HERE is a sum in mental arithmetic : How many pages are there in your Bible ? A thousand ? Twelve hundred ? Fifteen hundred ? Say fifteen hundred. Then a man has counted the number of times that flowers are mentioned in the Bible. They are spoken of three hundred times. Divide 1,500 by 300, and you find that, in every five pages that God writes, He speaks about flowers. Does that not show you how fond He is of them ?

Again, you know the story of God making Adam, the first man. Do you remember what was the first present He gave to him ? You might have thought that He gave him a house first of all, so that he would be safe from the wind and the rain ; or even a tent to protect him from the sun when it was very hot. But no. The first present was a garden. God meant *us* to love the flowers too.

There was once a man travelling across the hot desert of Africa, all alone, when a band of robbers came on him, wounded him, and left him half-dead. There he was, abandoned under the burning sun, with no friends, nor house, nor shelter near him. And there he lay down to die. Suddenly he started up. He had caught sight of a tiny green plant, a piece of moss, waving in the wind. " Why," he said to himself, " God is here looking after this small flower. He must be here to look after me too." He got up and struggled on, and, before night, he came to a hut where he was taken in and cared for. Now, after this service, these flowers you have brought will be taken to the old people, and the people who are ill. They will remind them that you are thinking of them. Better than that—they will remind them that *God* is thinking of them.

Next I want you to consider two things you have to do if the flowers are to grow in your garden :

1. You must put a wall round it. If you don't, you know what will happen. The cows, on their way to the market, will look in, and have a walk round, and a bite here and there. I know you are all very fond of cows—they give you cream to take with apple-tart—but you don't want to look out of the window and see a cow chewing your roses, or even sitting on the garden-seat. Nor is it only cows. There are rabbits that come in and eat the cabbages. And there are snails. I wish you could tell me of a wall that would keep out snails. They seem to climb the highest walls. And it's of no use to put broken bottles on the top. A friend of mine tried that, and he told me that one day he saw a snail, with its house on its back, sitting on the top of the wall, using a piece of broken glass as a mirror to see that its house was on straight. The snail brings its house with it. That means he has come to stay.

There is a wall round you, which God has put there to keep out the things that would spoil your garden. We call it the wall of Conscience. When you are going to do something wrong, you hear

God's voice within saying, " That is wrong : don't let that in." Try to keep that wall very strong.

2. Then comes the weeding. The cows and the rabbits and the snails are enemies from outside. There are also enemies from inside. If you don't get them out quickly they will choke the flowers.

There was once a man asleep in a tent, when a strange face looked in at the flap, and said, " Good evening, sir." " Good evening," said the man ; " I see who you are : you are a camel." " Yes," the camel said, " I am, and a very cold camel. Please let me put just my nose inside, till it gets warm." So the man allowed it to put its nose in. But next, it wanted to put its neck in, and then one leg, and then another, and then its hump. " This is too much," said the man. " Please go out and shut the door behind you." But it was too late. The camel only came farther in, till even its hind legs and tail were in. And then, as there was no room for both of them in the tent, the man had to get out.

Don't let temptations put even their noses inside. Turn them out at once.

Hymn

Here, Lord, we offer Thee all that is fairest,
  Bloom from the garden, and flowers from the field,
Gifts for the stricken ones, knowing Thou carest
  More for the love than the wealth that we yield.

Raise, Lord, to health again those who have sickened,
  Fair be their lives as the roses in bloom ;
Give of Thy grace to the souls Thou hast quickened,
  Gladness for sorrow, and brightness for gloom.

29

THE HIDDEN NAME

" I will give him a white stone, and in the stone a new name written, which no man knoweth saving he that receiveth it."—REVELATION ii. 17.

IN the book which tells about the conquest of Mount Everest, *First Over Everest*, you read this interesting story. Little was known about the geography of that country, and some adventurous men offered to go out exploring. They had to go into the forbidden lands of Tibet and Nepal and therefore they had to adopt a little pretence. They could not go under their own names, or they would be found out. So instead they took numbers. One of the most famous was an Indian. He was called Number Nine. He made some important discoveries. And he had another little pretence to make the work easier and less dangerous. He pretended that he was a doctor, travelling about to cure people of their sicknesses. He did really study his subject as well as he could in the time, and he had considerable success in his work as healer. He carried about with him a case of medicines given to him by some European doctors, and they told him carefully how to make use of the drugs. Each medicine had a number—they seemed fond of numbers in that country. And when Hari Ram (that was his real name) discovered what was wrong with any patient, he looked up his book of instructions and found which number of medicine to use. One day he was called in to the wife of a great chief. He found out what were her symptoms—where she felt the pain, and how she had no appetite, and so on—and, looking up his book, he saw that she needed some Medicine Number 19. But Number 19 was finished! What did he do? He wasn't at a loss. Nineteen, he pondered, is 12 plus 7. So he gave her one Number 12 and one Number 7. And I'm glad to say that, in spite of them, she was cured!

I wish I had known, when I was learning geography at school, that all these exciting adventures were met when men were getting the facts for our geography-books. I should have enjoyed geography much more than I did.

Here in the text God tells us that we shall have a hidden name one day. Not a number, for we come so late in the history of the world, that our number would be a very big one, millions and millions. It would be hard to remember it. But a name: we are to be, not just one of a crowd, but a special person whom Jesus knows and loves.

I believe that the hidden name which we are to get if we overcome is the name of ' Jesus.' When we come to the gates of Heaven and find them shut, we may be asked who we are and what we have done. Then, if we give our own name and nothing else, we shall not have much chance of getting in. There will be so many things marked down against our name that we might be kept out for ever. But, when they look at the white stone which God has given us and see there the name of Jesus, then the doors will fly open.

" I speak for them," Jesus says.   " They are under My protection ; they are Mine."

HYMN

O for a heart to praise my God,
  A heart from sin set free ;
A heart that always feels Thy blood,
  So freely shed for me.

Thy nature, gracious Lord, impart,
  Come quickly from above ;
Write Thy new name upon my heart,
  Thy new, best name of love.

30

PARADE OF BOY SCOUTS

" Thou shalt love the Lord thy God . . . and thy neighbour as thyself.
On these two commandments hang all the law and the prophets."
—MATTHEW xxii. 37–40.

As scouts, you have your splendid law, with its ten
commandments and its promise. If the law is broken,
the scout who breaks it is disgraced, and in him the
whole movement is brought into shame.

Let us look at this idea of law.

1. No human business can go on without it.
Think of the traffic in the streets. What chaos we
should have if there were no rules of the road! In
certain parts of the East there are none. In the
narrow, crowded bazaars, the drivers of cabs cry out
to one another to keep to the left or to keep to the
right, and naturally they often disagree, with disas-
trous results. The absence of traffic-law means confusion and the constant danger of accident. For ease
of movement and freedom from danger, you need
laws.

Lawlessness means confusion and grave danger.

2. You need rules in games. Cricket and football
and rugby all have their regulations, and an umpire
or a referee is there to see that they are kept. Without
them there would be chaos. But each player has
also a bundle of rules hidden away somewhere
within him, which he would probably call simply
' playing the game.' There are rules beyond those

which can be written down.   That is the second
point.

Laws are not from the outside but from the inside.

That means that no good laws can be looked on as
only a scrap of paper.   They are written in the heart
—if you break them, you destroy something that is
part of yourself.

3. You need laws in life.   Suppose that you decide
to become a doctor.   Then you will be called on to
take the doctors' oath, which governs their professional
life.   It is 2,400 years old, and it was drawn up by the
famous doctor Hippocrates.   It is the ' Scout Law '
of healing.   Here is one item of it.   If a doctor makes
a discovery of a new medicine or a new way of healing,
he must not keep it as a secret to himself.   He is in
duty bound to publish it.   It is not his own : it
belongs to the world.   He is not to keep it dark in
order to make money out of it.   His duty is not to
make money, but to heal men and women.   And here
is another item of the oath.   The doctor is to go
wherever he is needed.   It may be to a city scourged
with a terrible plague.   If he goes, he takes his life
in his hands.   But he must go, or he is breaking his
law.   He is not to run away timorously because he
wishes to save his own life.   That gives us the third
point.

Good laws are not from men but from God.

Or suppose you decide to go to sea.   You discover
a law governing the life of the captain.   He has a
rule on which he must act in case of emergency.   If a
storm threatens the safety of the vessel and he has to
abandon ship, he must not timorously regard his own

life. It may be very dear to him, as ours is to us. He may have a wife and children at home. But he must put these thoughts aside. He is to be the last to leave the sinking vessel. His first duty is to his passengers. Where does he get that law? Not from men. At first we may think so. When the *Titanic*, the finest ship in the world in her time, struck an iceberg and went down, many hundreds of people perished. At the inquiry a sailor was telling how they tried to rescue the women and children first. " I suppose," said the judge, " that is a rule of the sea?" "No, sir," was the answer; "it is a rule of human nature." He meant to say that not only sailors but all men everywhere would naturally think of giving the first chance of safety to the women and the children. Most of the people we know would probably agree with the sailor. But it is *not* a rule " of human nature." In the days of Julius Cæsar, for example, people would not naturally have acted like that. In Germany to-day the law is broken and dishonoured at every turn. And in certain parts of Africa no one would dream of considering the children first. We know what happens to the twins in Calabar. They are crushed into pots and so killed, or thrown out into the bush to be devoured by wild animals. " Women and children first " is not a law of human nature. It is a law which came into the world because of Jesus Christ. He taught that the strong are not to trample on the weak, but are to help them. And you have repeated His teaching in your own way, in your law, " A Scout is a friend to all "; " I promise to help other people at all times."

That is the third point about law. Good laws are not from men but from God. And this is the fourth :

Good laws are clear and simple.

No one could read your law and be in any doubt about the duty of a good scout. So with the law of the Old Testament. There we find ten commandments, perfectly clear-cut and plain. The pity was that the Hebrews were not content with that. They began to explain them, till the books of explanation filled hundreds of volumes, and the commandments were almost forgotten. When you have to multiply your laws like that, there is something far wrong. No man could hope to grasp the Jewish law in a whole lifetime. It was time to simplify. Micah did that in his famous words, " He hath shewed thee, O man, what is good ; and what doth the Lord require of thee, but to do justly, and to love mercy, and to walk humbly with thy God ? " If there had been Boy Scouts in the time of Micah, they might have taken that motto as their Scout Law. Jesus chose a simplification still more sublime. " Thou shalt love the Lord thy God, and thy neighbour." That is the whole law, He says. If we can live up to these two commands, we are what He understands by the word ' Christian.' To obey these two commands alone will take us a whole lifetime, all the strength we have, and all the help we can get from above.

There is something even simpler than this. You have your Scout Law, but you do not need to repeat the whole of the ten commands before you know how to act. You do it by a kind of instinct. You know what a good scout would do under certain circumstances. You have a pattern, and you would not require words. In the same way the Hebrews did not need to repeat the whole of the Ten Commandments before they could act. And a Christian to-day does not require to have the whole of the New Testament by heart before he can live a good life. He has what we call a conscience. Why do we obey conscience? Not very long ago a young student did a noble thing. He was sitting by the shore of the Moray Firth when he saw a boy who was swimming get into difficulties. Without a moment's hesitation the student did what a good scout would do instinctively. He made straight for the water and plunged in. He managed to seize hold of a plank, reached the boy, pushing the plank in front of him, and tried his hardest to get the boy on to it. The lad was exhausted and fell back again and again. To the very last the student persisted. At length he succeeded, and saved his man. But his own powers were exhausted. He sank and was drowned.

What makes a man do heroic deeds like this? It is something more than the words of the New Testament; something more even than conscience. What drives him on, even to giving up his life, when everything human within him cries out for life? It is the spirit of Jesus within him. Many of the finest deeds are performed by men who are alone, with no friends to hearten them and spur them on and inspire them. Companionship is a noble thing and makes a man capable of the finest actions. But even companionship may fail—unless it is the companionship of One who never fails. Jesus never failed anyone who trusted in Him.

You have your Law. And you have your solemn promise to obey the Law. But, best of all, there is the promise of Jesus, " Lo, I am with you alway, even unto the end."

HYMN

Be Thou my Vision, O Lord of my heart ;
Naught be all else to me, save that Thou art—
Thou my best thought, by day or by night,
Waking or sleeping, Thy presence my light.

Be Thou my battle-shield, sword for the fight,
Be Thou my dignity, Thou my delight,
Thou my soul's shelter, Thou my high tower :
Raise Thou me heavenward, O Power of my power.

31

SEVEN BROTHERS

I. SWORD AND PLOUGH

" *A land whose stones are iron and brass.*"—DEUTERONOMY viii. 9.

INTO that land, whose stones are iron and brass, came seven brothers of whom each took to himself three or four fields. Because the land was very rich they went to bed that night in great happiness. In the early dawn the first brother rose and ran out to dig in his fields and, in digging, brought to the light a rich piece of iron. He disappeared forthwith into the forest and was not seen for many days ; but when darkness fell there was the bright glare of a furnace among the trees, and far into the night the noise of hammering and the sharp clang of metal. When he returned he brought with him an odd pair of animals, a donkey and a camel ; between them was fastened his treasured piece of iron in the form of a plough. The others laughed loud and long ; but he turned unconcerned to his fields, coming home only when the stars looked out. And as he came he whistled merrily, as men do who plough in the fields.

The second brother also began to dig in his part of the land, and he too disappeared into the forest. When he returned he brought no plough, but in his hand was a sword and on his head a crown of iron and brass. Once more the others laughed boisterously, for their brother could scarcely lift the sword with both hands, and the crown was so heavy that in hot weather it made his head ache. (And, indeed, when no one was looking, he would hang it on a peg behind the door.) But he said to them, earnestly, " I have a sword and I have a crown : I'm going out to conquer the world. I shall get slaves to build me a palace ; and I have a mind to begin with you." But still the others laughed ; for his sword was heavy : before he could raise it from the ground they had run beyond his reach. Nevertheless, it was a sharp sword : if ever he grew strong enough to use it, it would mean danger. And now he put the sword on the back of a donkey and the crown on the back of another and strode away between them to conquer the world.

Years went past ; more years and more. Then one day he came back, tired and sad. His sword was no longer bright ; nor was it sharp now. He still had his crown, but it was battered and bent. The others came round to ask how he had succeeded. And he told them how the sword was so sharp that, once he had learned how to use it, he had conquered seven tribes and made them fight his battles and build his palace. And he was their king.

" But why did you come back ? " his brothers inquired.

" Because one day a man was brought before me for running away in battle ; and I asked him, ' Why did you desert in face of the enemy ? You are a brave man.' And his answer was, ' I ran from the battle because I am tired of fighting for *you* : I have a wife and I have children whom I love and I don't choose to be killed in your wars. I am brave enough to say that you are cruel and you are selfish and you are without a true friend in the world.' He said that to me ; and, when I heard it, I knew that I was a sham and a failure. I couldn't punish him : he had told only the truth. I remembered the happy times we had once here together, and one night I slipped away and left it all ; but I have brought the sword and the crown with me, so that they may do no more harm. I'm desperately hungry : have you anything to eat ? "

" Why, yes," they said ; " we don't lack for anything like that. You know how we laughed at our brother who made the plough. He didn't seem to mind, and every year he has ploughed his land and every year corn has grown up to make bread. We haven't been hungry for a long time now. Try some of his bread." And they were glad to see him again.

Hymn

Among the nations He shall judge ;
   His judgements truth shall guide ;
His sceptre shall protect the just,
   And quell the sinner's pride.

No strife shall rage, nor hostile feuds
   Disturb those peaceful years ;
To ploughshares men shall beat their swords,
   To pruning-hooks their spears.

32

SEVEN BROTHERS

II. THE BUGLER

" *A land whose stones are iron and brass.*"—DEUTERONOMY viii. 9.

HERE are the stories of the other brothers who found iron and brass in their fields instead of stones.

The third brother wakened one morning and said, " What shall I do with my iron and brass ?   Shall I build a palace and decorate it as palaces have never been decorated before ?   Or make an iron chariot and drive all round the world ?   Or invent a coat of mail that no weapon will ever be able to pierce ? Perhaps I shall do all of these ; but in the meantime these blankets are most comfortable : I'll have another snooze and make more plans to-morrow." And he rolled over on his other side and went to sleep. So the days went by, and the third brother did— nothing.

The fourth brother and the fifth rose up together one morning, for they were great friends, and, digging up a large quantity of iron and brass, they disappeared into the forest.   Night after night the others saw the glare of huge fires and heard the noise of hammering. Then the brothers returned, each carrying a sack. They had been making—money ! Bright, shining, brass pennies and little iron sixpences.   " Now to spend it ! " they cried, and off they set to the city beyond the horizon.

Late at night they came back. One looked tired and cross. He had spent all his money.

" And what have you brought back ? " his brothers inquired anxiously.

" Nothing," he replied. " I had the most wonderful things to eat, and I rode on all the circus-horses in the town. But one thing spoiled it all. When I was hurrying into the city there was a beggar sitting by the gate, poor and white and miserable ; and, when he begged from me, I pushed him aside, because I was in a hurry to enjoy myself. And I can't forget his hungry look."

" And what have *you* brought back ? " they asked the other.

" Nothing," he said. " Not an iron sixpence ; not a brass penny. I met a beggar too, poor and white and miserable ; and I thought to myself, ' Why, I can make money any time I like, and this poor chap has none.' So I took him along and gave him a good dinner. Ye buns and little pancakes ! how he ate ! And when he had finished at last he was quite a different fellow: happy; smiling all over; with colour in his cheeks ; just like a boy. So I whispered, ' How would you like a ride on a circus-horse ? ' ' Why,' said he, ' I haven't ridden on a circus-horse, not since I was *so* high : I could ride all afternoon on them.' And so he did ! I had just enough money to give him 121 rides and a supper at the end of it. And by that time he could ride so well and he fell off so seldom that they gave him a job in the circus. He will be able to keep his wife and family without begging any more. It was a grand afternoon ; and to-morrow I must make a lot more money, and see if I can find another beggar."

The sixth brother was quite different. No one liked him. Even his brothers found him hard to please, and the dogs all hated him because he usually had a stone in his hand. All that he made out of his iron and brass was a set of cruel traps for catching animals. His brothers pled with him to stop it, but he wouldn't listen. Then they destroyed all his traps; and he, in a fit of temper, strode away from home and walked on and on, till he came to a big city far over the horizon. And there he began to make cruel traps once more. When the citizens heard what he was doing they refused to go into his shop, and none but cruel people came as customers. One day three of these cruel people came in and asked him to make some long iron nails. And he made them. Next day, as he was walking on the outskirts of the city, he saw what they were using the nails for. They were using them to nail the feet and hands of Jesus to the Cross.

The seventh brother was only a boy; but he had watched his brothers using the forge, and he believed that he could make something too. What he made was a long, thin trumpet, or bugle. He couldn't play it very well at first, but every time he felt specially happy about this beautiful world, he put the bugle to his lips and blew one long, clear, lovely note. It was as good as a church-bell; for, whenever his brothers heard it, they bowed their heads and praised God for the wonderful world in which they lived.

HYMN

For the beauty of the earth,
    For the beauty of the skies,
For the love which from our birth
    Over and around us lies :
Christ our God, to Thee we raise
This our sacrifice of praise.

33

BIG MEN AND LITTLE MEN

" He was little of stature."—LUKE xix. 3.

SOME men are so big that they feel awkward about it. I know one who is so tall that when he goes on a sea-voyage he can never find a cabin-bed long enough for himself. (And a week or a fortnight is a considerable time to sleep with your knees touching your chin.) He tells me that he has always to be down early at the docks in order to get a cabin where the wall can be cut away to allow room for his feet. Another feels awkward because he is broad. One day a friend invited him for tea and told him to come by the Underground railway. But the big man inquired, " How can I go by Underground ? There is a turnstile at the entrance, and I am three inches broader than the gate." He had to try another way. The same man was once in a railway-station (it had no turnstile) and thought he would weigh himself to see exactly how stout a fellow he was. He stepped on to the weighing-machine, and hey presto ! the arrow rushed round at a tremendous pace as far as it could get, and then waggled backwards and forwards as if it would go a great deal farther if it could. He was two stones heavier than the machine could register. That is a fine picture of a little thing doing its best with a big problem. When you are little, that is all you *can* do—your best. But remember that big people can do no more than *their* best.

Little things can do a great deal. First, they can do a great deal of harm. When the world was very young, men used to have long battles with great wild beasts. They had to fight with bears and lions and tigers and elephants till they had conquered them and could live in safety. To-day men are still fighting with wild beasts, but mostly these enemies are tiny wild beasts ; so small that you could put thousands and thousands of them on a threepenny bit. (But you mustn't !) We call them germs, and it is these germs that bring diseases with them and kill so many people. In fact, I feel sure that it's not the big wild beasts of temptations, either, that are the most dangerous ; not the big sins that are like roaring lions. We can see them and we know when they are coming. It is the little wild beasts that are the real menace ; little sins that creep in out of the cold and pretend that they won't do much harm. We scarcely know they are there—and then, look ! the harm is done.

Happily it is also true that some little things can do great work for good. There was once a huge ship waiting to be launched in an English harbour. Crowds of people were there to see her take the water ; but something was wrong. The blocks and wedges were knocked away, but still the great hull did not move, and everyone was disappointed and alarmed. Then, to the amusement of the crowd, a small boy ran down and began to push with all his might and main. He had often launched his own boat by a good hard shove. Everyone laughed heartily at the idea of the boy making any difference. But suddenly they stopped laughing. The ship was beginning to move. It so happened that it had been just on the point of moving, and the pound or two that the boy could push made all the difference. The ship gathered force and soon was sliding gracefully down the slip-way into the water. He hadn't done it all, but he had done the bit that was necessary.

A little chap can launch a big ship. We can't all go about helping to launch ships ; but, if we keep our eyes open, there will be many times, every day, when we can lend a hand and do a kindness.

HYMN

The fields are all white,
And the reapers are few ;
We children are willing,
But what can we do
To work for our Lord in His harvest ?

We'll work by our prayers,
By the offerings we bring,
By small self-denials ;
The least little thing
May work for our Lord in His harvest.

34

THE ELEPHANT WHO BUILT A HOSPITAL

(HOSPITAL SUNDAY)

ELEPHANTS are hard workers. A man who has travelled much in the East tells me how he watched them piling up railway-sleepers. There were two elephants to each sleeper, one at each end. They would lift it carefully with their trunks, carry it steadily across the compound, and lay it on the pile. Then they would look along to see if it were straight (you could almost imagine that they were shutting one eye) and, if necessary, they would tap it into position with their trunks and turn back for the next. He said that they worked just as steadily as men, but they had one fault that men sometimes have also. Two elephants were walking along with a sleeper between them, and had gone about half-way, when the gong sounded to stop work for the day. Instead of finishing the job they were at, the elephants at once dropped the sleeper where they were and trotted off for their tea.

But it was not in this way that our elephant built the hospital. He didn't even carry wood for it but, without realising it, he did something which turned out even better.

Two men started on a journey, one from Scotland, the other from America. They were both hunters of wild animals. The American wanted to shoot as many big animals as he could and bring them home for a great museum. And he had plenty of money : some American millionaires were behind him and told him to spare no expense in making it the best museum in the world. The other went out to fight the smallest animals there were. He was a doctor and he wished to hunt down the fierce little microbes that bring diseases to men—so tiny that you can see these animals only with a microscope. (You don't need a microscope to see a lion or an elephant.) The doctor had not much money. He was sent out by the Church of Scotland, which gave him all they could, but they had no millionaires behind them. The two men arrived in the same part of Africa. The American went off after elephants, and, away up among the hills, very near the line of snow, he saw tracks of the largest elephant he had ever encountered. Unknown to him, a young elephant was watching. " I smell white man," it was saying, " come kill some of us heffalumps. Kill him first." Suddenly it dashed at the man. The hunter heard it coming and lifted his gun ; but the safety-catch had got damp and wouldn't move quickly enough. The elephant rushed. All the hunter could do was to seize its tusks as it came at him. The elephant came down with a savage wheeze, driving its tusks hard into the ground, thinking it had got him. " Him finished," it said to itself, pleased, as it galloped off to find his companions.

The hunter was knocked unconscious, and all his servants ran away, believing that he was dead. Some hours later he came round and shouted for help. One black boy came back and him he sent off with a message to his wife. The wife passed on word to the doctor—the only doctor within hundreds of miles.

Fortunately the doctor was able to find him in time and to look after him. He was very badly injured; but, with long care, he got better at last. When he was well again, he asked how best he could show his gratitude. The result was that he gave to the doctor a large cheque, enough money to build the hospital which was so badly needed for the African people in that district.

That is how an elephant built the Church hospital at Tumutumu. To-day the hospital brings healing to thousands of sick people; and, while they are there, they learn about the Gospel of Jesus who healed the sick.

HYMN

Father, whose will is life and good
    For all of mortal breath,
Bind strong the bond of brotherhood
    Of those who fight with death.

Where'er they heal the maimed and blind,
    Let love of Christ attend:
Proclaim the good Physician's mind,
    And prove the Saviour friend.

35

GREEN PASTURES

" The Lord is my shepherd ; I shall not want. He maketh me to lie down in green pastures."—PSALM xxiii. 1-2.

THE children of Scottish Sunday Schools maintain a bed in a certain hospital. We might call it 'The Hospital in the Hollow.' Imagine a big hollow dug in the earth, and at the bottom of it a lake. You have often read about it, for it is the Lake of Galilee. If someone were to dig a canal from the Mediterranean towards this valley, the water from the sea would rush in and drown everyone in the hollow. Beside the lake is this hospital. It holds the record of being the lowest hospital in the world.

For whom was it built? For the men and women and children of Palestine. They have no very good doctors of their own ; so we have sent out some of the very best from this country to look after them. They are not much accustomed to doctors, and they are not always in a hurry to go to hospital, even when they are really ill. They never like going alone ; so they wait till someone else takes ill too. Perhaps grandpa and auntie and the baby all turn ill about the same time. Then they go round the village asking, " Doesn't anyone else feel a little ill in here ? " Perhaps they find two others who need the doctor, and they say, " That's five of us. That's a good bunch. We'll all go along together. It will be cheaper, and better company on the road."

Many children come to the hospital. One of them was a boy called Mohammed. He was an Arab, and he came into the hospital very ill indeed. The doctors thought he had little chance of recovering, but they were determined to leave nothing undone. He used to be carried in on his mother's back to have his wounds dressed. It was a very painful business having his wounds attended to, but he didn't cry out, though sometimes the big tears ran down his cheeks. He was so brave that he began to get better. Every day he was a little stronger, and the nurses at last began to say, " Home again, Mohammed, some day soon ; but you must stay till you are quite better." Always he had the same answer. " Oh, please let me get home again before the *green* goes away ! " By the *green* he meant the green pastures of which we read. In Palestine you never see much green grass in the summer. It is only in the spring that the grass and the flowers can grow. When the hot weather comes, the sun burns them all up, and leaves nothing but sand and dust and wadies.

Every day Mohammed would slip away and climb up on to the window-ledge. There he would sit for hours at a time, gazing out over the streets below, seeing nothing of the busy village, but looking away to his own country. He knew what was happening away yonder. The spring had come and the grass was green again. All the flowers had come out and made the land like a rich carpet of colours. But the sun was gaining strength already, and he knew that, if he wasn't quick, it would all be gone again for another year before he got home. You can understand his longing to go back to his little tent before the green went away; once more to herd the goats in the green pastures; to roll among the green grass and the wild flowers. "Please," he would say again, "let me get home before the green goes away." And he got home in time.

I think we all have a longing like that. Jesus says, Come to Me before the green goes away : don't wait till your life is old and dry and dusty. Come when you are young and fresh and strong.

Hymn

Lord, in the fulness of my might,
  I would for Thee be strong :
While runneth o'er each dear delight,
  To Thee should soar my song.

I would not give the world my heart,
  And then profess Thy love ;
I would not feel my strength depart,
  And then Thy service prove.

O choose me in my golden time,
  In my dear joys have part !
For Thee the glory of my prime,
  The fulness of my heart !

36

FUN TO-MORROW

" I have learned, in whatsoever state I am, therewith to be content."
—PHILIPPIANS iv. 11.

SEPTEMBER is a difficult month in which to live up to this text. Summer is passing and winter is drawing on. Holidays are coming to an end and schools are beginning again. We feel the truth in the words of the wise man who said : " The best time for a holiday is the day after a holiday." It is then, we feel, that we need it most ! St. Paul would say, Learn to be happy all the time—happy on holiday and happy at home. For example, there was a girl four years old, whose summer holidays finished in the middle of August. She had to go back home when most of her friends were just half-way through their holiday. Someone sympathised with her : " Aren't you sorry to be going back to-day ? " But she tossed her head and answered, " No ; because I'm going home to my scooter ! " That was the right spirit.

I heard something of the same about a dog. He enjoyed being on holiday. It was his first train-journey. (The tunnel puzzled him. Night seemed to .come down so very suddenly. He wanted his going-to-bed biscuit. And then morning arrived again before you could turn round three times in the proper fashion and go to sleep.) And it was the first time in the sea. He couldn't understand the waves. At first he thought it was someone throwing a pail of water over him; and it had such a queer taste after the rivers in his south country. But he enjoyed the swimming and he had three long walks every day. It was a dog's paradise! You would imagine that he would mope on going back. But no. He ran everywhere with delight, for the pure fun of being home again. If the girl had a scooter to come back to, the dog had something just as exciting—a very special bone he had buried before he went away. For a moment he would sit deep in thought with one paw anxiously laid against his head, thinking hard, desperately afraid he had forgotten where it was buried. Then away he scampered and dug up—*two* bones !

There are many fine things we look forward to when we come back from holidays—the long winter evenings, and tea by lamplight; the cosy fireside and books; the robin's song in the garden and snow and Christmas; and starry nights (so much more beautiful because of the black-out) and sledging and skating.

Wherever you are, be content, says St. Paul. Why, we can't help it. God has prepared so many wonderful things for us to enjoy.

HYMN

Now thank we all our God,
With heart and hands and voices,
Who wondrous things hath done,
In whom His world rejoices,—
Who, from our mother's arms,
Hath blessed us on our way
With countless gifts of love,
And still is ours to-day.

37

HARVEST THANKSGIVING

*" Verily, verily, I say unto you, Except a corn of wheat fall into the
ground and die, it abideth alone ; but if it die, it bringeth forth much
fruit."*—JOHN xii. 34.

WHEN Jesus spoke these mysterious words, what did
He mean to tell His disciples ?   Let me try to put it
in the form of a story.

There was once upon a time a Mole, who lived in
a little house under the earth.   It was his habit every
day to have breakfast, and as soon as he had finished
breakfast to have dinner, and as soon as he had finished
dinner to have tea, and as soon as he had finished tea
to have supper, and as soon as he had finished supper
to have a short walk, and then to go to bed and dream
of all the fine meals he had had till it was time for
breakfast again.   Even as moles go, he was a fine
trencher-man : he had the best of appetites.

This day of which I am speaking, he had just
finished supper and was setting off for his short walk.
He took his walk under the earth—a way moles have
—and he had to make the road as he went along.   But
that didn't worry him, for he had a head shaped like
a wedge, and his nose was so sharp and so hard that
it cut a tunnel for him as fast as he could travel.

Now it happened that a farmer had been sowing
corn that day, and all the seeds had slipped down
into the ground.   Wherever the Mole went he ran
into hundreds and hundreds of these seeds ; and he

said to himself, What a waste !—to throw away good food like this ! I wish I were fond of vegetables, and I should have a glorious feast. But the Mole never eats anything but meat, so the seeds were of no use to him. It worried him, however. Every night when he went out for his walk he found the seeds tumbling to pieces. And he said again, What a stupid waste ! And in war-time too ! These seeds are all withering.

Then he went away for his summer holidays into another field and forgot all about them.

Many weeks had passed when he returned to the old field ; and the first thing that he noticed was this, that someone had been pushing a lot of silly little sticks down into the ground all over the field. To walk through the earth was like walking in a thick forest. Sticks everywhere !—and in his right-of-way that generations of moles had used from time immemorial. He didn't imagine that the sticks had any connection with the old seeds. What had happened, of course, was that the seeds had grown : up above it was autumn now and the field was covered with beautiful, tall, golden grain. But the Mole knew nothing of this : he knew only about the poor silly seeds that had lain there and decayed. Dead as a door-nail ! he exclaimed. A foolish waste !

Here is what Jesus meant by the text. " I am like a corn of wheat," He was saying to the disciples, " that falls into the ground and dies."

" What ! " the disciples cried ; " going to die ? You ? After all these happy years with us ? Die ! What a waste ! What a foolish thing ! " And

Jesus said very gently, " Ah, you mustn't be like the moles. If only you could get above ground and have your eyes opened, you would see the glory of the harvest."

To-day we can see it. All over the world there are Churches like our own, where people are trying to be good for the sake of Jesus ; and trying to help one another for His sake. A great golden harvest-field—and it couldn't have been there if Jesus had not died like the seed of corn. Thanks be to God for His gift of Jesus !

Jesus said that He was like the seed of corn. He had to die in order to do His work. He went farther than that. He thought of the bread that is baked from the corn, and He said, " I am like that too : I am the Bread of Life." Bread is the thing that we can't do without. If we hadn't that, we should die of hunger. That is why Jesus is the Bread of Life. Here is something that we *must* have if we are to live.

One thing more. Jesus knew how soon we forget. The disciples might even forget Him, though He had died for them. And He wanted to leave something by which they would be reminded. Again He chose the corn. They were having their last meal together : next day He would be put to death. So He took a piece of the bread on the table and broke it and passed it round to the disciples. " Think of this," He said, " as My body, broken for you. Whenever, after this, you sit at table and break bread, remember Me."

Four times a day we all sit down together at table and break bread. That means that Jesus wants us to think of Him four times in the day. If we do that, it will be a very good beginning. Whenever we break bread, then, let us recall the words of Jesus, " This do in remembrance of Me."

HYMN

By Christ redeemed, in Christ restored,
We keep the memory adored,
And show the death of our dear Lord
    Until He come.

His body, broken in our stead,
Is here in this memorial bread,
And so our feeble love is fed
    Until He come.

38

MISCHIEF-MAKERS

" They that seek my hurt speak mischievous things. But I, as a deaf man, heard not."—Psalm xxxviii. 12–13.

Some of the Scottish cities have interesting mottoes. Edinburgh (and also a famous Scottish regiment which was first raised in the city) has adopted the words from Psalm cxxvii. : " Except the Lord keep the city, the watchman waketh but in vain." (Perhaps you have seen the *Wakeman* at Ripon ?) Too often the motto of Glasgow is quoted only in part : the end of it, the most important, is missed out : " Let Glasgow flourish *by the preaching of the Word.*" Carved on one of the monuments in Dumbarton are the fine words, " Just wecht : fear God." But it is of a motto which comes from Aberdeen that we are reminded by this text. It runs, *They say : what say they ? Let them say !*

" They say." That means that there are always people who talk slander and pass around gossip. They speak mischievous things. " They say "—we can see them whispering behind their hands, saying things behind a person's back that they would not dare to say before his face. And that is always a wicked thing to do.

" What do they say ? " That suggests that the things which are whispered are never true. If they were true, people would be brave and say them openly. Mischief always spreads, and grows as it spreads.

We used to have a game, when we were preparing to go abroad as soldiers, a game which gave great fun, and also showed how slander could easily be spread. We used to play it during night-operations. It was practice in passing messages along a line. The message began at one end, and was passed from mouth to mouth. Long before it reached the other end of the line, it was usually changed into something entirely different. For example, the man at one end would begin the message, *Enemy in sight ! Send up 50 bombs.* And, along at the far end, it would arrive : *Could do with a bite : send up 50 buns.* Or an officer would dispatch the message : *Send reinforcements : am going to advance.* At the other end it would come out : *Send me three-and-fourpence : am going to a dance.*

I have been told of a comical one which is supposed to have happened in actual battle. A battalion had advanced towards the enemy at night and were in an exposed position where the only cover was found in the shallow pits which the men had painfully scraped with their entrenching-tools. The officer wished to find out if the enemy were near at hand, and passed along the message that he was going to send up a Véry light, or light-rocket : *All crouch down : I'm sending up a flare.* Along it came to the extreme end of the line : *You're all to kneel down : the officer's going to put up a prayer.*

If urgent, necessary and innocent messages can be so completely changed on the way, you can readily understand how slander spreads, and grows as it spreads.

Of course, there may be some little grain of truth

in it. There was once an old Greek gentleman who was so happy that he used to go along the streets singing. And the boys used to laugh at him, for he could not sing very well. " There goes old Anaximander," they would cry, " singing out of tune as badly as ever ! " The old man heard them once, making fun of his singing ; but, instead of flying into a temper and chasing them with a stick (which they deserved), he simply said, " I dare say there is some truth in what they say, or nice boys would never say it. Then I must learn to sing better." And off he went to take some lessons. When people speak mischievous things, that is the best way to stop them. Put right what is wrong, and then they have to stop.

Far more often, there is no truth whatever in what is said ; and that is where the third part of the motto comes in. " Let them say ! " Let them speak mischievous things. I am as a deaf man : I hear not. That is the best plan.

From the motto part has been dropped out, just as in the case of Glasgow ; and, once again, it is the best part. Originally, the motto ran : *They say : what say they? so ye do weel, let them say.*" That is splendid and true. If you have done nothing wrong, talk cannot hurt you in any real sense. Let them talk : you can be as a deaf man and hear nothing.

That is the plan which Jesus Himself adopted. We read that His enemies made up all kinds of evil stories about Him. They knew very well that they were false, and everyone else knew. Jesus answered nothing. He was as a deaf man, as one who hears not. " Answerest Thou nothing ? " they asked Him.

" What is it they witness against thee ? " But Jesus held His peace.

What say they ? *So ye do weel, let them say.*

HYMN

Through good report and evil, Lord,
Still guided by Thy faithful word—
Our staff, our buckler, and our sword,—
    We follow Thee.

Strengthened by Thee we forward go,
'Mid smile or scoff of friend or foe ;
Through pain or ease, through joy or woe,
    We follow Thee.

39

ALL KINDS OF MUSICK

*" What time ye hear the sound of the cornet, flute, harp, sackbut,
psaltery, dulcimer, and all kinds of musick."*—DANIEL iii. 5.

ONE summer I had a musical holiday. Next door
there was a family of three, a big girl, a big boy, and
a very little boy. The big girl played the piano, very
fast. She wanted to have all her pieces practised at
lunch-time so that she might get out for a game in
the evening. The big boy played—a cornet! He
played it always at tea-time, and very slowly, so that
you found yourself holding your tea-cup half-way to
your mouth and waiting for the next note. The
little boy played in the morning on a comb wrapped
round with tissue-paper (but he called it his cornet-
flute-harp-sackbut-psaltery-dulcimer); and he played
best of all, for he played tunes that no one had ever
heard or played in the world before.

In the same town there is a museum which has a
most surprising organ. It has three manuals, the
first of pieces of slate; the second of steel plates; the
third of bells. The men who invented it travelled all
over the country giving demonstrations, and once
they played before Queen Victoria. They even had
their photographs taken.

More interesting even than that is a small set of
slates, discovered by a stone-breaker. He had a fine
ear for music, and he always listened for the ring as
his hammer hit a musical slate. In this way he picked

out eight of them to make an octave, and set them up carefully on a board with felt mats. At first you might think there is nothing less musical than a piece of slate. (You know what the sound is like when you draw your slate-pencil across it !) It needed a sensitive ear to discover these musical slates, and to put them in their right setting.

Jesus is always listening to your life. If you have any fine music at all, He will hear it, and put you just in the right place for it to be heard.

He has to *play* the music too, if it is to be heard at its best. There was once a small girl who was very fond of music, but she had not much opportunity of practising, for in the house there lived a cross old man who was annoyed when she played *Home, Sweet Home* with one finger on the piano. It happened that a great musician was coming to stay with them for a little, and the girl was told that she must keep out of the way. He was coming at ten o'clock that night, and he wouldn't be bothered with small girls. In the afternoon she went up to the room with the piano to play for the last time before he came. Down below, in the drawing-room, they heard the little tinkle of a melody. It was *Home, Sweet Home*, staccato, with one finger. Then, suddenly, rich, beautiful chords were woven round the notes, and the whole house was filled with the harmony. The great musician had come earlier than was expected and was leaning over her shoulders, helping with the music. That is what God does with the little tunes we play in our lives. So long as we play our best, He leans over us and brings out of it all a beautiful harmony that makes everyone wonder.

" All kinds of musick." There is the grand music of Heaven which only God can play. And there are the little tunes which we can play. But the finest of all is heard when we play the best we can, and God pours the music of Heaven into it.

HYMN

Holy Spirit, hear us ;
    Help us while we sing ;
Breathe into the music
    Of the praise we bring.

40

THE DONKEY

"*And when the ass saw the angel of the Lord, she fell down under
    Balaam : and Balaam's anger was kindled, and he smote the ass with
    a staff.*
"*And the Lord opened the mouth of the ass, and she said unto Balaam,
    What have I done unto thee, that thou hast smitten me these three
    times ? "*—NUMBERS xxii. 27-28.

BALAAM was going away on a journey.   God had told
him *not* to go, but Balaam, thinking that he knew
much better, just stopped his ears and clenched his
teeth and closed his eyes and went.   He thought he
was getting on splendidly, till the donkey stopped,
and refused to move an inch.   Balaam thought it
was pure stubbornness and he struck it ; but a few
yards farther on it stopped again, and lay down.
Balaam could see nothing in the path, but the donkey
saw, quite clearly, an angel.   God wanted to show
Balaam that with all his pride he wasn't half so clever
as his own donkey.

I expect you know the poem in which a donkey
tells about his own life.   He was born, he says, in a
queer time, when fishes flew in the air, and trees
walked about on the land, and figs grew on hawthorn-
bushes.   Everyone laughs at his monstrous head,
and his silly bray, and his long, foolish ears that look
like wings.   Everyone, he says, beats him and makes
fun of him.   But he has a secret, and he can afford
to smile at it all :

137

Fools ! For I also had my hour,
  One far fierce hour and sweet :
There was a shout about my ears,
  And palms before my feet.

You know what he was remembering—that day, many years ago, when Jesus rode in triumph on the back of a donkey, and the people scattered palm-branches before Him. Ever afterwards, the country-people say, the donkey carried the sign of this. Look at his back, and you will see that he wears a long, dark cross—the sign of Jesus.

We mustn't laugh at the donkey or—if we can't help that—at least we mustn't be cruel to it. Once it saw an angel when its rider could see nothing ; and once, on a memorable day, it carried Jesus on its back.

There was a time when another donkey became famous in history. It was in a law-court, where there were rows and rows of ugly benches in a dusty room ; where men were reading long passages out of dusty books ; where everyone was very learned and very sad. A case was being tried, and the day was so warm and the room so hot that many of the men were asleep, when the door opened and in walked—a donkey ! It had come to be a witness ! Everyone was wide awake at once. And everyone laughed. But the donkey won. A society had just been formed to see that no one was cruel to animals. The man who started that society was Richard Martin : he was so good to animals that he was called ' Humanity Dick.' This was the first case they had found, since the society came into being, of deliberate cruelty. A man had been thrashing his donkey till it was covered with sores; and Martin had brought the donkey into court to show the truth. The donkey won!

It was because Jesus chose a donkey to ride on, that memorable day outside Jerusalem, that people at last began to understand that we must be good to animals.

HYMN

Ride on! ride on in majesty!
Hark! all the tribes " Hosanna! " cry;
O Saviour meek, pursue Thy road
With palms and scattered garments strowed.

41

JEROME AND THE LION

" Overcome evil with good."—ROMANS xii. 21.

ST. JEROME lived about three hundred years after
Jesus ; and, because he loved Jesus so much, he
went to live in Bethlehem, where Jesus was born.
Perhaps the most famous thing he ever did was to
translate the Bible into Latin. That may seem a
strange thing to us, for we find it hard enough to read
a few short sentences in Latin ; but then Latin was
the language that most people understood best in the
time of Jerome. If you had been at school some time
ago, you would have spoken Latin very well too.
You would have had to speak it in class instead of
English. And that is why we still have some Latin
words connected with school. Sometimes you hear
a school-teacher spoken of as ' the dominie.' *Dominie*
is just the Latin word for master. And sometimes,
I think, you still say *pax* when you are making up a
quarrel. ' Pax,' of course, is the Latin word for
' peace.' And sometimes you say *cave*, meaning
' Look out ! Someone coming ! ' ' Cave ' is just
Latin for ' beware ! ' In some parts of Scotland the
schoolboy's word for punishment by the teacher's strap
is *pandy*. ' Pande,' in Latin, means ' Hold out your
hand ! '

How glad we should be that we can read the Bible
in English, which is to us the familiar tongue which
Latin was for most people in the days of Jerome.

We owe our English Bible to the fine scholars who translated it for us many centuries ago.

What these scholars did for their age, Jerome did for his time in the little cave at Bethlehem. There is a famous picture of him at work in his study; and beside him is a huge lion, asleep like a dog at his feet.

One evening, when Jerome was sitting with the other monks around him, a strange visitor walked in. It was this huge lion, limping with pain as he walked; because he had a wounded paw. The other monks ran away in terror; but Jerome stayed. He went forward and welcomed the lion to the monastery, and began tenderly to look after its sore paw. The lion was very grateful; and, instead of running back again into the forest when its paw was better, it remained, wanting to do some work for this kind man.

Every day an ass was sent out from the monastery to bring in the wood for the fire and the task which Jerome gave to the lion was to look after the ass in each day's foraging; to take it out in the morning and to bring it back in the evening. For a time all went well; but one day, when it was very hot, the lion lay down for a quiet snooze and, while it was asleep, some merchants came along with a string of camels, and, seeing no one with the ass, they walked off with it. When the lion wakened up and saw that its companion was gone, it began to roar as only a lion can roar. But all in vain. The merchants only hurried off the faster. At last the lion went back to the monastery and lay down sadly outside the gate, ashamed to go in, because it had lost its friend whom it was supposed to look after. When the monks noticed this, they said at once that it must have eaten the ass ; must have fallen back into its old, fierce habits. (If you once get a bad name, it is very hard to make a good name for yourself again.) Jerome was the only one who still trusted the lion. The others would not give the animal any food, but said to him, " Go away and eat what you have left of the poor ass." Then they made the lion, day after day, do the work of the ass and carry the wood for the fires. This work the lion performed very meekly, but it never forgot its old friend, the ass.

One day, when the lion had an hour to spare in the afternoon, it set off to try whether it could find its friend again. It roamed round the district in a wide circle and at long last saw a caravan approaching. To its joy, it was the merchants who had stolen the ass ; and there, right in front of a dozen camels, was the old companion. The lion let out such a roar of welcome that the merchants took to their heels and disappeared. Then the lion came joyfully home, leading the ass and the camels too (for he didn't know what else to do with them). He was no longer ashamed, but ran happily into the monastery, crying as well as he could with a roar, " See what I've brought home for tea ! "

Shortly afterwards, the merchants came to ask Jerome's forgiveness for having stolen the ass (and perhaps, too, to see if they could recover their camels). They fell on their knees before him, and Jerome treated them with great kindness. " Take back what is yours," he said ; " but do not touch what is not your own." They were so thankful not to be punished that they gave him a present of oil, and promised that every year they would send some more. The lion and the ass became closer companions than ever after that, and worked happily together for the monastery.

The text for the story is in four words—" Overcome evil with good." The lion is just a person with a bad temper ; and the best way to overcome that is to be gentle. It takes two to make a quarrel. And the merchants are just bad, dishonest people, cured by a good example.

Hymn

(O Jesus, I have promised)

O let me hear Thee speaking
  In accents clear and still,
Above the storms of passion,
  The murmurs of self-will ;
O speak to reassure me,
  To hasten or control ;
O speak, and make me listen,
  Thou Guardian of my soul.

42

THREE PRINCES

Characters :

The King.
The Three Princes : Alexander, *the eldest.*
                    Philip, *the strongest.*
                    Peter, *the merriest.*
The Council of the Ten Great Thinkers.
Brachys, *Officer of the Council.*
First Servant.
Second Servant.

Prologue

[Brachys *engaged preparing the Council Chamber for its final meeting ; setting ten chairs in a semi-circle round the table facing the audience, and one larger chair in the middle of the semi-circle. He places fresh sheets of foolscap, long quill-pens, and ink-bottles at each place, taking away the old sheets and commenting on them.*]

Brachys : Ten days they've been at it, talkin' and thinkin', thinkin' and talkin'—and sometimes just talkin'. Even forgettin' to take their food. And *that* means somethin' serious. And most of ten *nights* they've been at it and all. They seems to sleep with one eye open—and the other only half-shut. And always write, write, writin' with them birds' fevvers. Give *me* my fevver-bed ! *And* the paper that's wasted. Here's a pretty picture ! (The young ones does *them* : they're too young yet to talk, let alone think, so they passes the time scribblin' notes and drawin' pretty pictures.) *That's* a good horse now! Except that it hasn't but three legs to walk on. 'Twill do for my little boy. Make him more contented like with his own wooden pony. It has to go without a tail, but it *does* have the right number of legs.

And here's a pretty ship at sea! Ah, but they'll be sick, sick, sailin' at that angle and longin' for home, they will. And the mice has been gnawin' at the sails.

[*Enter* COUNCILLORS 1 *and* 2. (*Bearded old men.*) *Exit* BRACHYS.

FIRST COUNCILLOR : Things weren't so hastily done when I was a lad. Choosing the heir to the throne was a long business then. Seventy-five days my father sat in this same Council Chamber. All meals brought in ; and hearty eaters they were. And beds provided.

SECOND C. : Wooden beds too ! So my father used to say. They're best for the brain. " Hard beds, hard thinking."

[*Enter* COUNCILLORS 3 *and* 4 (*even longer beards*).

THIRD AND FOURTH C., FIRST AND SECOND C. : Good morning !

THIRD C. : Our last meeting.

FOURTH C. : And a hard nut for the young princes to crack.

FIRST C. : Nice boys too, all of them.

THIRD C. : I'd be happy with any one of them as my King.

FOURTH C. : A pity we can't have them all.

SECOND C. : Four months each, turn and turn about !

[*Enter* COUNCILLORS 5, 6, *and* 7. *They are young men, rosy-cheeked and clean-shaven.*

FIFTH C. : Five minutes before time ! Not so bad for the younger generation !

SIXTH C. : I should have been late as usual, but the cook dropped a frying-pan and wakened me up. I thought it was the gong for breakfast.

SEVENTH C. (*gathering a handful of quills from a stand in the centre of the table*) : These quills are very sharp. They must be uncomfortable for the birds that have to wear them. (*5, 6, and 7 begin to play darts with the quills, using a sheet of foolscap as target.*)

[*Enter* COUNCILLORS 8 *and* 9 (*still longer beards*).

EIGHTH C. (*sees paper pinned up as target*): Ah ! A royal proclamation ! (*Adjusts spectacles on his nose.*) What's this ? What's this ? You young rascals !

NINTH C. : Boys will be boys ! (*Tries a throw at the target. Loud applause if he hits it, which is unlikely.*) Boys will be boys !

EIGHTH C. : And old men should know better !

[*Enter* NUMBER 10, *the Scribe. He carries a large roll of parchment under his arm—the Minute Book. And he has the largest beard of them all.*

TENTH C. : To business, gentlemen ! To business ! Ah, a proclamation !

"Whereas . . ." They always begin like that, but I can't see beginning or middle or end. (*Sees the others laughing,* NUMBER 8 *most of all.*) Scoundrels all of you ! (*Pulling* NUMBER 8 *by the beard.*) And the bigger the beard the bigger the scoundrel ! (*Sud-*

146

denly recollecting himself.)   Your places, gentlemen !
The King is on the way.

FIRST SERVANT (*announcing*) : His Majesty the King !
(*All rise.   The* KING *enters and goes to the middle
chair.*)

KING : Pray be seated, gentlemen.

Gentlemen of the Council of the Ten Great
Thinkers, We have been informed already of the
substance of your wise deliberations.   The Scribe
will now read at greater length the report of your
counsels together.

THE SCRIBE (*reading from the Minute Book*) :
" Whereas the Council of the Ten Great Thinkers
was summoned by command of His Majesty the
King, and Whereas it was laid upon them, according
to the ancient custom of this Realm, to arrange and
set forth a Scheme, Plan, or Device, whereby His
Majesty the King might the more readily choose
for himself an Heir and Successor, according to
the ancient custom of this Realm,

The said Council of the Ten Great Thinkers did,
and hereby does, suggest, propose, and submit, for
the consideration of His Majesty the King, this
Scheme, Plan, or Device, the outcome of their
sober and diligent meditation, as followeth here-
under,—

Firstly, To each of the three princes there shall
be granted the sole use of one room in this palace
to be his own for the period of one year and one
day ;

Secondly, Each of the aforesaid three princes shall
be required to fill the room appointed to him for

his use with such article, commodity, or possession as shall appear to him the most precious in all the world.

Thirdly and Lastly, His Majesty the King, on his return from the frontiers of his Kingdom, shall be graciously pleased, according to the ancient laws of this Realm, to decide and determine among the three."

So please Your Majesty.

KING : Then, Gentlemen of the Council, our business is complete. To-morrow morning we ourselves shall explain your plan to our three sons. On our return, after a year and a day, we shall appoint as heir to the throne the prince who has responded most wisely to your test. Adieu.

[*Exit, attended with all due ceremony.*

ACT I

(*Next Morning*)

Curtain rises on a sunny morning-room. The THREE PRINCES *are playing some children's game. The game begins to flag.* . . .

ALEXANDER (*sleepily, because of the heat*) : Why do socks have clocks ?

PHILIP (*also sleepily*) : I don't know. Why ?

ALEX. : To show whose they are. By looking at the clocks, you can tell which are *hours*.

PHILIP (*rather scornfully*) : Ha, ha ! And, if socks have clocks, clocks should have socks.

PETER : Perhaps they have. They have faces and hands, so they ought to have feet. And feet mean socks.

PHILIP : It's far too hot for conundrums.

ALEX. : It's too hot to think.

PETER : *I'd* like to take off my skin and sit in my bones.

ALEX. : What does Father want with us to-day ? I meant to ride out on my new pony under the trees. He was a bargain at a hundred pounds. He'll walk in any moment now.

PHILIP : Your pony ?

ALEX. : No, Father.

PHILIP : And did you say that Father was a bargain at a hundred pounds ?

ALEX. : If that's another conundrum, I'm asleep.

PHILIP : *I* meant to sit all morning in the tree that hangs over the river and trail my feet in the water. It's wonderful to think how the water that tickles my toes is running on to turn the mill-wheels, and then out to sea to carry the ships to the end of the world. Peter, if ever you go to sea, look at the waves and think that they were tickling my toes a week before they reached you.

PETER : *I* meant to bury poor Solomon.

PHILIP : O bother your old lizard !

PETER : He wasn't an *old* lizard. He was only seventeen.

PHILIP : But he died of old age.

PETER : Yes, he died of old age all right ; but he took it just the day before.

[*Enter the* KING.

149

KING : Good morning, boys. I have a special matter to speak about. I leave to-morrow for a tour of my Kingdom. You will be good boys while I am away?

PHILIP : How long will you be away, Father?

KING : A year . . .

PHILIP : A year!

KING : . . . and a day.

PETER : A year and a day!

ALEXANDER, PHILIP and PETER (*together*) : It's a long time to go on being good!

KING : Well, well; do your best—if you can! (And your worst, if you dare!) But here is the special matter. I want to know who is to be heir to the throne. By the laws of our land, he need not be the eldest (*looking towards* ALEXANDER), nor the strongest (*looking towards* PHILIP), nor the merriest (*looking towards* PETER); but he *must* be the wisest. After many days and nights of consultation, the Council of the Ten Great Thinkers have devised a test. You will each be given a room in the palace to be your own, to do what you like with. And, before I return, in a year and a day, you are to fill the room—fill it quite full . . .

PHILIP : Smoke!

KING : . . . with the most precious thing you can think of. . . .

PETER : Toffee!

KING : . . . And whoever does it best will be king after me. Be good boys, and try your wits. Good-bye!

THE PRINCES : Good-bye.

[*Exit the* KING. *Sound of horses, jingle of harness. The* PRINCES *wave from the window.*

CURTAIN

ACT II

(*A year and a day later*)

SCENE 1

The KING *and* PRINCE ALEXANDER

KING : Well, boy, and what have *you* done ? Something very wise from the eldest prince ?

ALEX. : Yes, Father ; I hope so. I've worked hard for a year and a day, and I think you'll be pleased.

[*He opens the door of the first room, disclosing floor, table, chairs, etc., covered with gold, silver, and precious stones.*

KING : Riches ! Gold, silver, precious stones ! You have been very diligent. . . . But the room was to be *filled.*

ALEX. (*sadly*) : Yes, Father, I remembered ; but it takes a long, long time. The gold ran out, and I tried silver. When the silver was finished, I gathered the precious stones. But think, Father, of the things we can buy with all this !

KING : What things ?

ALEX. : It will buy land—broad fields and rich pastures !

KING : Yes, it will buy land—from those who will sell. Anything else ?

ALEX. : It will buy honours.

KING : Honours, yes ; but not honour. Not *real* honour. A great soldier once said that he could capture any city in the world if the gates were big enough—big enough for him to drive in a mule laden with gold. Yes, gold may buy a city, and for silver men will sell their honour. But, Alexander, you cannot buy the honour which you and I love.

ALEX. (*quietly*) : Money will buy friends.

KING : Friends ? I wonder ? In my journey I often needed friends, but I travelled alone. All knew that I was a rich man, yet none came about me save beggars and flatterers and slaves. But one day I was alone and in danger. That day I found a friend. And he would take *no* reward. Adventure wins friends ; and need and danger ; good friends ! But money, never ! Money, well used, is powerful ; but, in the things that matter most, money is helpless. One day, as I rode near the sea, a child had fallen over the cliffs. I had plenty of money in my saddlebags. (A stout rope had been better !) But, while we all stood, the father came, and, breaking through the crowd, he clambered down the precipice and brought the child back in his arms. Love will win when wealth stands idly by. Should *you* be king after me, Alexander, build not your kingdom on riches, but on love.

CURTAIN

SCENE 2

The KING *and* PRINCE PHILIP

KING : Your room, now, Philip. Have you *filled* it ?

PHILIP : Yes, Father.

KING (*smiling, as he remembers*) : With smoke ?

PHILIP : No, Father ! Something more precious than smoke.

[PHILIP *opens the door of the second room.*

KING : Bravo ! Filled with the scent of flowers ! Well done ! That is a precious thing. There is memory in the scent of a flower. Far, very far away, I once found a bunch of wall-flowers growing in a lonely place ; and, in a moment, I was back at home, a child again. They say that sheep and cattle, being carried across the sea, weary of the ship which is their prison, are the first to know that land is near. They feel the scent of grass and flowers far out at sea.

You have filled the room. And with a precious thing. But yet—it fades. It lingers, yes ; but it perishes at last. Yet this was a wise and lovely thought. The kingdom may be yours. If it be so, will you promise to build your kingdom on the things that perish not ?

PHILIP (*softly*) : I promise !

KING : Your mother loved us. And she is dead. But love cannot die. It is for ever and ever.

CURTAIN

SCENE 3

The KING *and* PRINCE PETER. *The scene should be played very slowly.*

KING : And now, my small mite, how have you fared ? (*Playfully*) Is it toffee ? A mountain of nougat ? Fifty-two Saturday pennies-worth of treacle ?

PETER : No, Father ; I filled the room with the first

penny, and I couldn't think of anything that would make it better.

KING : Lead on !

[PETER *opens the door of the third room.*

But everything is dark. Is this one of your merry tricks, little one ?

PETER (*goes to a box in the centre*) : My lizard Solomon had died just before you went away. This is the box he slept in—all lined with felt to keep him warm at night. And I got a candle with my penny. (*Lifts the box : the candle shines out merrily.*)

KING (*softly*) : Filled ! Every nook and cranny filled !

[*Meditatively, while* PETER *kneels by the box, shading the candle with his hands, on the side away from the audience. As the* KING *speaks,* PETER *slowly drops his hands and looks up at his father, listening very intently.*

Most worthily and wisely did you choose.

Not wealth but light !—which money cannot buy.

Poor men or rich, the sun is for them all.

And yet *all* wealth is there. The brave, blue sky ;

The colours of the earth ; the flowers ; the face of friends—

Light gives them new with every dawn of day.

Most precious light ! Most sweet, majestic light !

When first God filled the world with joy, and gave

The symbol of His presence and His care,

He said, " Let there be light ! "

(*Slowly*) " Let there be light ! "

Most worthily and wisely did you choose,

My little son, my little king-to-be !

SLOW CURTAIN

43

THE VIGIL

" A watch in the night."—PSALM XC. 4.

You might imagine that this was the watch which you put under your pillow at night; or one of those watches with luminous paint on the face that shines in the dark so that you can tell the time without switching on the light—" a watch in the night." But you know that there is another kind of watch—a guard, a look-out, a sentry. There used to be a conundrum when I was small : " Who was the smallest man who ever lived ? " The answer was, " The man who slept in his watch." (Look at Isaiah lvi. 10.) He would have to be *very* small to curl up in his watch and go to sleep. But of course it was the other kind of watch in which he slept—at a time when he ought to have been awake, alert, on guard.

You remember a sad story of three men who slept in their watch. Jesus had taken His three best-loved disciples, just a few hours before He was captured and put to death. He wanted them to wait and keep guard while He was praying. But, when He came back, He found that they had fallen asleep. And He said, sadly, " Could you not watch one hour ? " Perhaps, if they had been strong enough to keep awake and to watch, they might have shown up better. As it was, when the crowd came to capture Jesus, they lost their heads; tried to fight their way out; then took to their heels and ran. Jesus was left alone. Had they watched, they might have kept cool and stayed with Jesus to the end.

An artist has painted a striking picture called ' The Vigil.' The word means ' The Watch.' It is the picture of a young man holding up his sword before the altar in a cathedral. He is to become a knight next day, and it was the custom to spend the hours of darkness in prayer. He is consecrating himself and his sword to the service of God.

That is what you are doing when you come to Church; when you come to Sunday School; when you kneel down to say your prayers. You are keeping watch with God in His temple. If you do that, often and often, one day—you will see God! If you are often there, in God's temple, a wonderful thing will happen. God will come into *your* temple. His best temple, the one He loves most, is a pure heart.

Hymn

Blest are the pure in heart,
  For they shall see their God;
The secret of the Lord is theirs;
  Their soul is Christ's abode.

Lord, we Thy presence seek;
  Ours may this blessing be;
O give the pure and lowly heart,
  A temple meet for Thee.

44

OWNING THE SKY

" He went away sorrowful : for he had great possessions."
—MATTHEW xix. 22.

IT seems a strange thing to be sorrowful about—that you have great possessions ! Not many people are sad because they are rich ! This must have been a very attractive young man. Jesus loved him, we are told ; and he came to Jesus anxious to learn as much as he could from Him. Then he found there was one thing in the way—his money. It came to be a struggle between his possessions and Jesus ; and his possessions won. The trouble was that he forgot that they were all God's ; that he had them only for a short time.

I suppose that none of you is likely to be sorrowful because you have too many possessions. What have you got all to yourself ? Your school-books for one thing. But perhaps you scarcely reckon them as riches. Then probably you have a cricket-bat or a tennis-racquet ; a stamp-album or a collection of wild flowers. And I hope you have something alive— a goldfish, or tadpoles, or a kitten, or a puppy. Ah ! you say, but these are very small things. But then you have a great many possessions besides these. Who owns the roads, do you think ? Why, you do. They belong to the nation—that is, to you and me. And the public parks ? You and me again. And the picture-galleries ? Sometimes people leave a famous

picture to the nation—that is, to us, you and me
once more. We have a vast number of great
possessions.

Who, do you think, owns the sky? It looks as if
you and I come into the picture once more. We can
fly a kite in it, and no one will stop us. How much
of the sky do we own? I'm not quite sure. The
nations are claiming to-day that the sky above their
own land belongs to them and to no one else, so that
aeroplanes, even when peace comes again, must ask
for special permission in order to fly over other
territory than their own. It may be that this is the
right way of looking at it. The whole of the sky is
God's; but He has given to everyone a bit to look
after.

If that is so, you see what it is leading to? If you
have a garden—and I hope you have, no matter how
small it is—then you own far more than the little
space of the soil bounded by the garden-walls : you
own all the sky above it, right up to the stars ! In
fact, it goes farther than that—it goes right up to
God. All our possessions are like that. We possess
them for a little time, but they all belong to God—
flowers and hills and gardens ; goldfish and kitten
and puppy :

> All things bright and beautiful,
>   All creatures great and small,
> All things wise and wonderful—
>   The Lord God made them all.

HYMN

Let all the world in every corner sing:
    " My God and King ! "
The heavens are not too high,
His praise may thither fly ;
The earth is not too low,
His praises there may grow.
Let all the world in every corner sing:
    " My God and King ! "

45

INFLUENZA

" Let your light so shine before men that they may see your good works, and glorify your Father which is in heaven."—MATTHEW v. 16.

WE have been hearing a great deal about influenza : some of us have even been having it. It is a funny big word, a hard word for a hard thing. And it has a queer meaning. It means ' influence,' and that is just something that ' flows in.' For one of the first points you notice about influenza is that it is ' catching.'

Most badness is catching. If one has it, another is apt to get it too. Think of a bad habit, how it spreads from one person to another ; it has an ' influence.' Or think of a mischievous boy in a class : before he has been there many days, all the boys begin to turn mischievous.

But I am glad to say that goodness is just as catching as badness. You know the charming song written by Longfellow about the arrow and the song. He shot an arrow into the air and thought it was lost. But, many years afterwards, he found it, still unbroken, sticking in an oak-tree. And once he had sung a song and forgotten all about it ; but, long, long afterward, he heard the song come back to him from the lips of a friend. The friend had not forgotten : the song had cheered him up, and it was stored for ever in his heart. (Be very careful, when you sing that song, not to mix up the verses and so plant the arrow, not in the oak-tree but in the heart of your friend.)

Badness is like influenza : it is catching. And goodness is catching also. So are good deeds. Let men see them, the text says, and they will soon begin to *do* them. We all have influence, for good or for evil.

Once, in a big and busy city, they wanted to build a church for the poor people who lived round about ; but they had no money with which to begin building. They asked for subscriptions, but some had very little money to give ; and some who had the money wanted to use it for other things : building a church was the last thing they would do with it. At last the church-people decided to give out collecting-boxes. They asked the people in the neighbourhood to put in as much as they could spare every week. Even though it was only threepence or sixpence, it would mount up in time. One day there came to the hall a very small girl with a very white face, and asked for a box. The superintendent looked at her, and said to himself, " This tiny girl hasn't enough food for herself. She oughtn't to be giving away money, even for a church." And he said to her : " You are too small, my dear ; wait till you grow up, and then you'll have a box all to yourself." But the girl said, " Perhaps I'll never grow up ; could I please have one now ? " She pled and pled with him ; and she was so determined that at last he gave way, and she went off proudly with her box.

Not many weeks afterwards, the minister in the district received a message asking him to call at the house of this same girl. She was whiter than ever. She was very, very ill. She had never in her life had enough to eat, and now it was all having its effect. The minister could see that indeed she was not likely to grow up. She was too weak to speak, but she was always pointing to the window. He wondered what it could be that was attracting her attention. Did she want to see the sky?—a tiny square of blue could be seen between the roofs if you looked at the proper angle. But it wasn't the sky. Then he caught sight of the collecting-box standing on a shelf beside the window, and he held it up. Was it this? The girl nodded. He took it over to the bed. She was too weak even to open it, but she signed to the minister to do that. He opened the slot at the foot, and shook it. Out fell two half-pennies. It was her contribution to the church that she would never see. The minister was wondering if any of them would ever see it, for the subscriptions were not coming in fast; but more than ever now, and for her sake, too, he hoped that some day it would be built.

Next Sunday morning his mind was so full of the little girl's splendid contribution that he couldn't help telling his congregation about it. He described her poor home, and her starved body, and her shining eyes when she gave him the two half-pennies. In the vestry afterwards, a stranger came in to speak to him. "Was that a true story you told," the stranger inquired; "or did you just invent it to help the subscriptions?"

"It was a true story," the minister said; and he went on to tell the stranger more about the girl.

" Would you excuse me a moment ? " the stranger asked, when the story was told. He went over to a desk in the corner of the vestry, took out his fountain-pen and wrote a line or two. Then he handed it to the minister, who saw that it was a cheque. " My contribution for the building of the church," the stranger said ; " but it doesn't mean as much for me as the two half-pennies meant to the girl."

The minister found that it was a cheque for £3,000. The church was built without any more trouble. Two half-pennies had made it possible.

" Let your light so shine before men that they may see your good works and glorify your Father which is in heaven."

HYMN

The wise may bring their learning,
    The rich may bring their wealth,
And some may bring their greatness,
    And some bring strength and health ;
We too would bring our treasures
    To offer to the King ;
We have no wealth or learning ;
    What shall we children bring ?

We'll bring Him hearts that love Him ;
    We'll bring Him thankful praise,
And young souls meekly striving
    To walk in holy ways :
And these shall be the treasures
    We offer to the King,
And these are gifts that even
    The poorest child may bring.

46

MAKING PULPITS

" I heard the voice of the Lord, saying, Whom shall I send, and who will go for us? Then said I, Here am I; send me."—ISAIAH vi. 8.

THAT morning Isaiah went into Church, all by himself. There was no service going on, but he wanted to pray for his nation; someone was needed to help his country. And, as he prayed, he heard an unexpected thing. He heard God saying, "What about you? Will you go?"

When God called, he could not refuse. The call may come to any of us. When it came to David Livingstone, many people were surprised. One man, who knew him as a boy, said, "David is just a quiet, feckless sort of boy." But Livingstone knew that God was willing to take him just as he was and to make him what He needed.

Perhaps there were other things that Isaiah had longed to do; other things he would rather have been than a minister. Many have felt like that. Mr. Struthers, once minister in the Scottish town of Greenock, when he was a young man, was offered an excellent post in Australia at £600 a year—a very great deal of money for a young man in those days. He refused. People said to him, in astonishment, "Will you reject this offer, to become a Cameronian minister at £80 a year?"

"I cannot help it, sir," he replied; "I have made up my mind to be a minister." God had called him: he could not refuse.

Not everyone can be a minister; but all can work for God. There was once a small boy who was watching the joiners working in his house. He loved to see the chips flying and the shavings curling off the wood, and the saws and the hammers and the chisels at work. And he made up his mind there and then to be a carpenter when he grew up.

"I hope," someone said to him, "that you will look higher and be a minister."

But someone else said, "Jesus was both."

Then the boy himself added, "I'll be a carpenter *and I'll make pulpits* !"

Whatever our work is, we can serve God. Do you know the story of the three stone-cutters? They were working on a block of stone. A stranger asked the first what he was engaged on. The man answered, "I'm earning ten shillings a day."

He asked the second.

"I'm cutting this stone," he replied, with a bit of a growl as if it were very exhausting work.

The third, when he was asked the same question, "What are you doing?" answered, "I'm building a cathedral."

That man had the secret.

HYMN

Just as I am, Thine own to be,
Friend of the young, who lovest me,
To consecrate myself to Thee,
    O Jesus Christ, I come.

I would live ever in the light,
I would work ever for the right,
I would serve Thee with all my might,
    Therefore to Thee I come.

47

ONLY A SPARROW

" Are not two sparrows sold for a farthing? and one of them shall not fall on the ground without your father."—MATTHEW x. 29.

WHEN the smallest sparrow falls out of the nest, God sees and cares. We take it usually as a sign of God's sorrow for the bird. But perhaps it is sometimes a sign of God's anger? Perhaps it has been some person's cruelty that has thrown the young bird to the ground? Then God must be angry.

They say that it happens even in this country—that tiny birds are found, thrown out of the nest and killed, and the nest torn down. We can hardly believe that it is done by boys. It must surely be evil spirits dressed up in boys' clothes.

" It's only a bird! " these evil spirits say. If they say that, they are not fit to live in this land; they belong to that dark, pagan land where birds are killed because people think that God likes to have them sacrificed to Him; where worse things happen, for the people often put a boy to death in the same way.

" It's only a boy," they say; " who cares? "

" Only a bird! Only a boy! "—but God made them both.

Outside a church near Oxford is a notice which rivets your attention. We often see something very like it: Please shut the door. But this is put in an unusual and beautiful way. It is not a request to keep out the dust from the church ; nor to keep out the draught nor the rain nor the sheep. It is to keep out the birds—and for a special reason. This is how it runs :

Pray, of your charity, to close the door, lest any little bird, entering, should die of thirst.

That is a fine thought to have in church—in a place where we worship God who cares for the sparrows as well as for men and women, girls and boys. Close the door, or a bird might fly in and be left there, when you are gone, with no chance of reaching the stream for a drink ; to die slowly of thirst.

God cares for the birds. We must never be cruel to them. They do more than sing for us. Sometimes they have given their lives for our sakes. Many a time, during war, it is necessary for men to go down into a shaft or mine. It might be full of gases. They might never come up again, but be stifled down there. And one way of testing the air is to send down a bird first. Again and again when these cages have been pulled up, the bird has been found dead. It has given its life for its country. In Edinburgh Castle, in the noble War Memorial of Scotland, you will see to-day a special monument to the birds that gave their lives in this way.

" Only a bird ! "—but a creature of God and a friend of men.

God must love the birds very much, for it was to them and to the angels that He gave wings.

HYMN

All things bright and beautiful,
  All creatures great and small,
All things wise and wonderful—
  The Lord God made them all.

Each little flower that opens,
  Each little bird that sings,—
He made their glowing colours,
  He made their tiny wings.

48

THE HUMAN TELEGRAPH

" And the Word was made flesh, and dwelt among us."—
JOHN i. 14.

THIS is a story of *Talking versus Doing*.

In the orphanage that morning there was considerable excitement, for a wealthy Countess was coming to pay a visit. Some of the boys, unfortunately, did not know how important a person a Countess was ; and, when she came into their room, they were in the middle of a fight ! They were quarrelling over a book. It was *Robinson Crusoe*. There was only one copy in the house and they all wanted to read it at the same time. They were scrambling and fighting so hard that they failed to hear the visitor come in. The Countess was shocked to see them pummelling one another so heartily, and she asked what it was all about. Then the matron tried to make an excuse for the boys. She explained that there were hardly any books in the library for the boys to read, and, as they were all very keen on reading, there were frequently long struggles to get possession of the few books they had.

The Countess thought to herself, How nice it would be to give them a present of all the books they want. But she was a very busy lady. She had to attend so many parties that the whole business went quite out of her head until many weeks afterwards. One evening she was in the house of the Chief Counsellor and someone happened to mention orphanages. The Countess remembered then ; and, because she wanted to say something in this clever company, she told about what she had seen.

The Counsellor thought for a little, and said certainly they should send some books for the boys. In fact, he recalled that he had a large trunk full of books at home, which his children used to read before they were too big. However, when the company had gone, he decided that it was too much bother to go rummaging over the house for an old trunk : he was too important a man to waste his time on that.

Nevertheless, he was dining next evening with a friend, an important statesman ; and, as he wished to please him, he told the story of the orphanage. He added that, in his opinion, books ought certainly to be sent to the boys.

" Nothing is simpler," said the statesman ; " to-morrow I am going to the office of the newspaper ; and I shall see that a notice is put in its columns asking for books to be sent."

When he arrived, he discovered that the newspaper was looking around earnestly in every direction for something exciting to put in its columns. This was the very thing. The chief reporter sat down at once and wrote a moving article about the poor little tots with nothing to read. Then he went home, whistling, to his dinner.

A few days later, two people stood outside the locked door of the newspaper-office. One was a shabbily dressed old man, with very grimy hands ;

and the other a pale, thin little girl, carrying a bundle of books.

" These," said the old man, " are for the children you wrote about." They took a little time before they remembered about the orphanage, and then they inquired his name. They said they must put it in the papers, so that people would know who had given the books.

" Oh, but that isn't necessary," the old man said ; " I'm only a poor man working in the factory : I just wanted to help the children." And he went off with his thin little daughter.

The story is called *The Human Telegraph*. I think you can guess why. A message for help had gone out from the orphanage. The answer came from far away in the factory. All those in between had done nothing but pass it on to someone else. They were just *telegraph-poles*. All of them had talked a great deal. They had all said, " Something must be done." But it was words only, until it came to the old man and the girl. They had no words, but they were there with the books. They had come themselves.

That brings us to the text. In the season of Advent we remember " The Word became flesh." God wanted to help the world. He *might* have sent a message to someone else asking if they would care to help. But He didn't do that. He came Himself, bringing the help that was most needed.

HYMN

We give Thee but Thine own,
  Whate'er the gift may be;
All that we have is Thine alone,
  A trust, O Lord, from Thee.

To comfort and to bless,
  To find a balm for woe,
To tend the lone and fatherless
  Is angels' work below.

49

HOLLY IN THE HEART

" Man looketh on the outward appearance, but the Lord looketh on the heart."—I SAMUEL xvi. 7.

How does God manage to see our heart? It is so far inside us. Well, we must remember the wonderful things that even men can do to-day. You have heard of the marvellous thing called the X-ray. Suppose that a soldier has a bullet in his body, and the doctor is not quite sure where it has gone ; he turns on this strange ray, and then he can see right in among the man's bones and muscles, where the bullet is lying concealed. The text speaks of *God's X-rays*. He can see farther than bones and muscles : He can see the heart, and that is the part which matters in the eyes of God.

I once read a sermon preached on this text—not by a minister, nor by a teacher, but by a man who didn't even know that he was preaching. He was a taxi-driver in London. It was Christmas-time, and there was a great deal of traffic in the streets. Some of the drivers were losing their tempers. There was one in particular, the driver of a motor-lorry. He was very proud of himself. He had a beautiful big lorry and he had decorated it that morning by putting a bunch of holly on the bonnet. He was so proud that he thought he was the best driver in London : everyone else should make room for him. So, when the taxi-driver was held up by the traffic and couldn't get out of the way, the lorryman began to shout names at him and to call him the world's worst driver. But the taxi-man got the best of it. He looked down at the bunch of holly and said :

" What's the use of 'aving 'olly in yer bonnet, if you ain't got 'olly in yer 'eart ? "

That's just it. What is the use of putting up holly for Christmas, if you haven't got the spirit of Christmas in your heart ? It's not Christmas yet, but it is the time when parties are beginning. There will be a lot of new and lovely party-frocks ; but that is not the important matter. God likes to see your party-frock, but what He is really looking for is the party-spirit. That means that you are not out simply to enjoy yourself, but to make everyone else enjoy themselves. What's the use of having a party-frock if you haven't the party-feeling inside ?

It is also the time when winter games approach the most exciting stage. You have your football-jersey, and you are proud of belonging to a team. But the important matter is not to look like a player : it is to have the player's spirit. You know the kind of boy who plays for himself all the time. When he gets the ball he won't part with it. Even when he is running straight into the opposing half-backs he won't pass, though the man on the other wing has a free run for the goal. He wants to score himself : he doesn't care what happens to the team, so long as he gets some credit. There's no point in having the team-jersey on, if you haven't the team-spirit in your heart.

" What's the use of 'aving 'olly in yer bonnet, if you ain't got 'olly in yer 'eart ? "

Man sees the holly on the bonnet : God sees the holly in the heart.

"Man looketh on the outward appearance, but the Lord looketh on the heart."

HYMN

Gracious Spirit, Holy Ghost,
Taught by Thee, we covet most,
Of Thy gifts at Pentecost,
   Holy, heavenly love.

Love is kind, and suffers long,
Love is meek, and thinks no wrong,
Love than death itself more strong ;
   Therefore give us love.

Faith and hope and love we see,
Joining hand in hand agree ;
But the greatest of the three,
   And the best, is love.

50

WITHOUT MONEY AND WITHOUT PRICE

(CHRISTMAS IN THE PRIMARY SUNDAY SCHOOL)

ONCE upon a time there was a small boy who went with his father to buy Christmas presents. All sorts of wonderful things his father bought—books and sweets and toys—to send away to children in the lands where there is no Santa Claus.

While his father was busy, the boy saw a little ticket on the counter. He could only just read and he made out, Please Take One.

" What does that mean, Daddy ? "

" It means that you can have that for nothing."

That was fine, and the boy took one ; but it wasn't a sweetie, nor a toy, nor a book : it was only a bit of paper with writing on it ; not even pictures. And the boy thought : You don't get much for nothing.

They went into another shop—a shop which had lovely things in the window. There were apples and oranges and story-books ; and a train with a steam-engine and a station and signals.

" Daddy, can I take one of these too ? Is this one of these Please Take One places ? "

" No ; I'm afraid you have to pay for these."

Every morning, when the boy was going to school, he used to stop in front of this window, and press his nose against the glass, and look at the apples and the oranges and the story-books and the train. But he couldn't buy any of them. The train cost pounds! And the books cost more shillings than he had ever seen! And even an orange cost twopence. He felt in his pocket. He knew that he had only a half-penny, but he thought that he would make sure. There was plenty in his pocket, but it wouldn't buy an orange. There was a marble, and a bit of a cracker from the party last week, and string—plenty of string —and a pencil, and a bit of rubber, but no more money; only the lonely half-penny.

One morning he went forward to press his nose as usual against the glass, just for another look when— his nose went right through!

The glass was gone. And there on the fruit was the notice Please Take One. And on the story-books was the notice Help Yourself. And even on the train was a notice Given Away for Nothing.

And then he knew that he must be dreaming. There aren't any shops like that in all the world!

I wonder! There are some splendid things you get for nothing. To begin with, there's *you*. You didn't have to pay for yourself. God gave you yourself all for nothing.

And there are your father and mother. You didn't have to go to a shop and say, " I want a nice Daddy, please; a pretty cheap one, because I haven't got many pennies." You didn't have to look at one after another, trying to get one a little cheaper; or take one that was a little soiled through being in the shop a long time so that you got him for less. You didn't have to say, " I see that Mummies are very expensive to-day: I'll come back when there's a sale on or when I've saved up a little more." You just got them for nothing at all !

And the best of all—God's Christmas present to you at this time. You don't have to pay anything for that. All for nothing, you can have Jesus for your Friend, without money and without price.

HYMN

Away in a manger, no crib for a bed,
The little Lord Jesus laid down His sweet head.
The stars in the bright sky looked down where He lay,
The little Lord Jesus asleep on the hay.

51

SPIDER THREADS

" She hath done what she could."—MARK xiv. 8.

WHEN all the toys are off the Christmas-tree; when we have all had our presents till next year comes round; when the candles are all burned out, there is still something left on the branches. We call it *tinsel* —little ropes of silvery stuff twined in and out of the twigs. Their name comes, through the French, from the way in which they sparkle. They aren't for eating and they aren't for giving away. They're just there! Perhaps you know what they stand for? They stand for spiders' webs.

The first Christmas was over; and, instead of rejoicing, there was crying. Herod, the king, had sent his soldiers to kill all the children born about that time in the country. He had been told that one of them was going to be king, and he was afraid for his own throne.

> Thou art a soldier, Herod! send thy scouts,
>   See how he's furnished for so feared a war.
> What armour does he wear? a few thin clouts.
>   His trumpets? tender cries. His men, to dare
>   So much? rude shepherds. What his steeds? alas
>   Poor beasts! a slow ox and a simple ass.

The mother and father of Jesus had been warned by God; and, taking their little son, they went off across the plains towards Egypt. All day and all night they travelled; and, when the morning broke, Joseph thought that they were safe at last. Mary and the child were very weary, and he chose a roomy cave where they might rest for an hour or two.

It was very cold in the early morning, and a little spider which happened to be in the cave was sorry for the baby, with no warm bed and no warm blankets. It wondered if there was anything it could do to help. There was only one thing, and that seemed very little. He could spin a web. "Perhaps," he said, "it will keep out a little of the cold air and the wind : I'll spin my web right across the door of the cave." So he span his web, and very beautiful it looked when the dew formed on it and sparkled in the sun. Perhaps it didn't keep out the cold very well, but he did what he could.

Joseph himself had dropped off to sleep too. He thought that they were far out of all danger now. But, while he slept, there appeared on the horizon a line of camels. It was a company of Herod's soldiers who had heard of the escape of this child and, taking the swiftest of the camels, had set off in hot pursuit. What if they should find the cave and look inside ? They came nearer and nearer. One of them spied the cave and cried, "Perhaps they are hiding in here." He made his camel stop and kneel down, and he was swinging himself out of the saddle when he noticed the spider's web across the entrance.

"Ride on," he cried ; "it's all right ; no one has come in here ; there's a spider's web right across the door."

And on they rode, till they disappeared again over the horizon. The spider's threads had saved the life of Jesus. And that is why we hang the tinsel over the Christmas-tree. He did what he could. He thought it was a very little thing, but it saved the Holy Child.

Some day God will ask of each of us, " What did you do down there on the earth ? " Some people will be able to say, " I did this great thing and that great thing," but, when it comes to our turn, perhaps we shall have very little to say. But that will not matter if we can answer God's question with two wonderful words ; if, when He asks us, " What did you do ? " we can look up and answer " My best."

Hymn

In the bleak mid-winter,
  Frosty wind made moan,
Earth stood hard as iron,
  Water like a stone ;
Snow had fallen, snow on snow,
  Snow on snow,
In the bleak mid-winter,
  Long ago.

What can I give Him,
  Poor as I am ?
If I were a shepherd,
  I would bring a lamb ;
If I were a wise man,
  I would do my part ;
Yet what I can I give Him—
  Give my heart.

52

GOING HOME

" I have finished the work which Thou gavest Me to do."
—JOHN xvii. 4.

ON Christmas Day I listened to a fine sermon. It was a very short one—only nine words ! And it was preached by a very short boy. He was a milkboy, carrying round his bottles of milk on the outskirts of the city. We wished each other a Happy Christmas, and then I said to him, " You'll be getting home earlier to-day to have a holiday." This was his answer and his sermon : " I'll get home," he said, " when my work is done." That was the right kind of boy. With him it was work first, and only then did he think about holidays.

The second thing I can put best in a story : In a sleepy little town in England there lives an old man who walks with a limp. He was a sergeant in the South African War. One day, as he was riding with a troop of cavalry from one British post to another, they were fired on by a clever ambush of the Boers. The sergeant was badly wounded and fell from his horse. The others made off to the nearest block-house to bring help. All but one. He was a boy who had just left school and come straight out to the front as a lieutenant. He stayed with the sergeant to tie up his wounds. The Boers opened fire again. At this the boy put himself between the wounded man and the enemy, shielding him with his own body. In a moment he was wounded in twenty places and his blood poured over the other man. The sergeant saw that his rescuer was dying. " Oh, how sad ! " he said, " that you who are just setting out on a brilliant long life should die for me—an elderly man of no importance in the world." The officer turned to him with his last smile. " Sad ? " he exclaimed ; " what could be better ? " And he fell back dead. The boy had gone home—but his work was done. He had performed a great work—more perhaps than any of us will be able to do in the longest life—and performed it in a moment.

" I have finished the work which Thou gavest Me to do."

Hymn

O God of Bethel, by whose hand
    Thy people still are fed ;
Who through this weary pilgrimage
    Hast all our fathers led :

Our vows, our prayers, we now present
    Before Thy throne of grace :
God of our fathers, be the God
    Of their succeeding race.

O spread Thy covering wings around,
    Till all our wanderings cease,
And at our Father's loved abode
    Our souls arrive in peace.